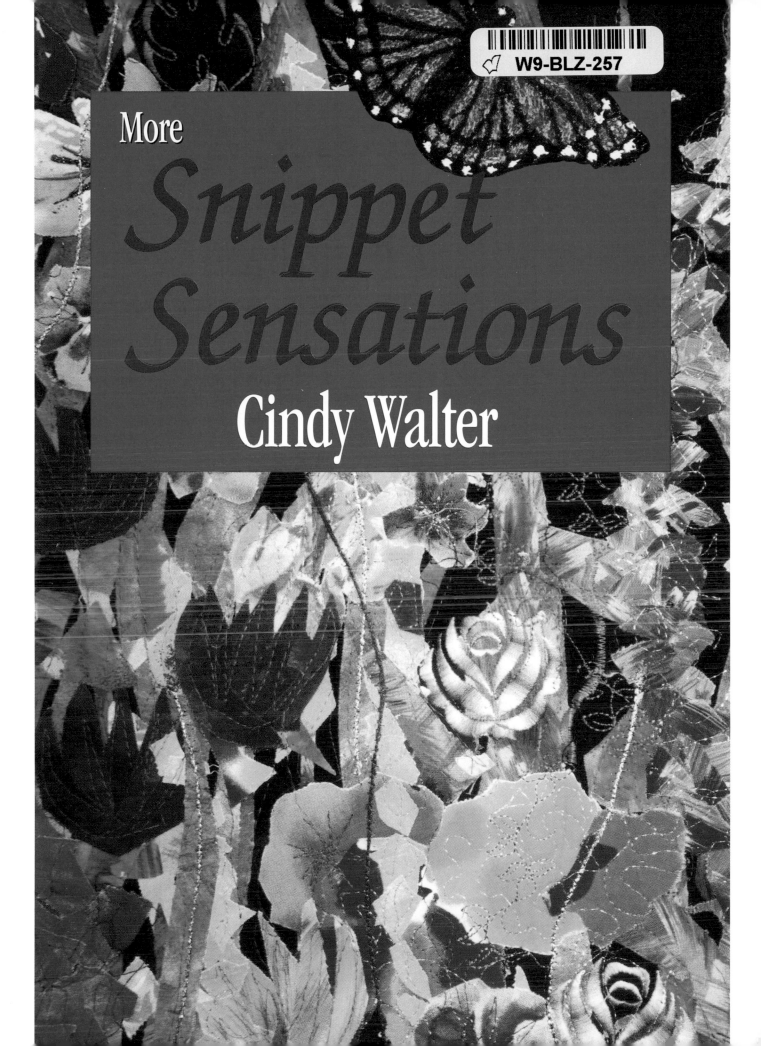

More

Snippet Sensations

Cindy Walter

Published by

Krause Publications
700 E. State Street
Iola, WI 54990-0001
Telephone: 715/445-2214

Please call or write for our free catalog of publications. Our toll-free number to place an order or obtain a free catalog is 800-258-0929 or please use our regular business telephone 715-445-2214 for editorial comment and further information.

Library of Congress Catalog Number 99-69494
ISBN 0-87341-915-4

Unless otherwise noted, photography by Mark Frey, Yelm, WA, and Kris Kandler and Ross Hubbard, Krause Publications, Iola, WI.

Table of Contents

Featured Works

(Alphabetical by title)

*Denotes that step-by-step instructions are included.

Author's Introduction

Quilting is my favorite pastime, and I am deeply committed to keeping traditional quilting techniques alive. The techniques passed down to us by our elders are a very important part of this country's heritage. Two of the books I co-authored this year with Diana Leone, *Fine Hand Quilting* and *Attic Windows* (shown below), promote traditional quilting. I alternate between creating and teaching both traditional and contemporary quilt styles, and I especially enjoy teaching and encouraging students to create their own unique designs.

Autumn Trees, 29″ x 21″, 1995, by Cindy Walter. *This is the first Snippet project I made. I added the cherry red leaves a year after I "finished" it.*

I often spend my free time designing new quilts. This is how Snippet Sensations began. One night, I was lying in bed with insomnia. My brain was busy thinking of a new twist for my quilts. I wanted to create one that looked like a Monet painting—*I was thinking about actually painting on a quilt*. What would I use to paint on the quilt? Fabric paints? Acrylic paints? Then it came to me: paint *with* fabric. I could cut pre-fused pieces of fabric up into little bits, like dabs of paint, and apply them to my quilt. The next morning (before making coffee—this shows how eager I was) I put the concept to the test by creating my first Snippet quilt, Autumn Trees (at left). Wow! My idea worked, and it was so quick and easy! I couldn't wait to begin another Snippet project!

In 1995, after months of experimenting to develop the technique and teaching it to workshop students, I wrote *Snippet Sensations*. Since then, it has been rewarding for me to sit back and watch my work plant the seeds of inspiration in others. This effortless technique has swept the world. Needless to say, Snippets have taken over my life (and the floors of my workroom). Since the publication of *Snippet Sensations*, my life has been in a whirlwind: I have taught quilting around the world, appeared on numerous TV shows, and spent endless hours writing new books.

I'd like to thank my friends and family for their constant support and to the readers who have sent me letters and snapshots of their Snippet projects that were inspired by my first book. I appreciate the photos and your exciting, encouraging stories. Thank you to Diana Leone, for her input in Part III, to Amy Tincher-Durik, my dedicated editor at Krause, and to all of the artists whose works truly make this a beautiful book.

Welcome to my world of Snippets. May your own "fabric painting" be sensational, and may it bring you and your loved ones a great deal of joy.

Cindy Walter

Introduction

Snippet Sensations, also called Fabric Art, means to freely cut pieces of fabric to create a picture. The snippets can be small dabs or large sweeping panels, random or specific shapes. The essence of the Snippet technique is freedom. If you need a circle, cut a circle, and if it isn't round, it is better. A fusible web is first applied to the back of the fabric pieces so once the picture is finished, it can be permanently fused into place.

This book will teach you how to create your own unique Snippet Sensations masterpiece. The quilts and other projects are here to inspire your creativity. A supply list and individual instructions are provided for more than 20 of them. Please read the General Instructions section (Part II) carefully because this information applies to every project in the book.

The five parts of this book will guide you through the Snippet technique:

Part I introduces you to the world of Snippets, including a glossary, overview of the technique, and a summary of the supply list.

Part II provides the general instructions. This section helps you select the needed supplies and teaches the Snippet process. There are many choices in the technique, including supplies, background style, and types of fabrics to use. Reading this section completely allows you to make the best choices for your projects.

Part III covers how to turn a Snippet project into a quilt. This section includes tools and supplies needed for machine quilting and binding the quilt.

Part IV is a Snippet gallery. Use the quilts and projects in this section for inspiration. The captions point out unique features; study the pieces' design, depth, and color.

Part V has step-by-step instructions for more than 20 projects, including quilts, garments, and framed artwork.

I knew Snippet Sensations was popular when I saw this cartoon by Don Tyler, which appears in his book, Show & Tell 3 *(EPM Publications, Inc.).*

PART I

Overview

*T*his section introduces you to the world of Snippets. It includes a glossary and basic supply list, as well as an overview of the technique. It is important that you read this section before beginning any of the projects featured in this book.

Glossary

Foundation fabric. The piece of fabric used as a base on which snippets or panels of fabric are adhered to create the Snippet project. This can be compared to the canvas on which an artist paints. The foundation fabric can be completely covered with snippets or panels of fabric, or it can be exposed as a part of the design.

Fusible web. A two-sided fusing film used to adhere two pieces of fabric together by ironing, rather than sewing. Also referred to as webbing and appliqué web.

Palette fabric. The fabrics used to create the design images. These fabrics are first attached to fusible web and then cut into snippets or panels.

Pre-fuse. To adhere fusible web to the wrong side of fabric before you cut it into smaller shapes. Some brands of web use the heat of an iron to pre-fuse, while others are pressure-sensitive and can be temporarily attached to the fabric without ironing.

Snippet Art or Snippet Sensations. Terms I invented for projects created with pre-fused pieces of fabrics that are freely cut into random or predetermined shapes and then fused onto a foundation fabric.

Snippets. Pre-fused fabric cut into snips or shapes. There are four types of snippets:

    Panels. Large pieces of pre-fused fabrics used for larger predetermined shapes such as mountains.

    Predetermined-shaped snippets. Pieces of pre-fused fabric cut into a specifically planned shape such as a square or fence post. For the most part, these predetermined shapes can be freely cut without predrawing. Occasionally, you may want to draw the shape on the web's paper liner and then cut it out as with an appliqué pattern.

    Random-shaped snippets. Shapes cut from the pre-fused fabric in a free, unplanned, arbitrary shape.

    Theme snippets. Theme fabrics have images printed on them. Pre-fuse theme fabric and cut around the edges of the images to add them to your project. For instance, to add a fish to an ocean scene, simply cut out the fish from pre-fused printed fabric. This is also known as fussy cutting.

Panels.

Predetermined-shaped snippets.

Random-shaped snippets.

Theme snippets.

General Supply List

*Design source
(a drawing)*

Here is a brief list of the supplies you *may* need for a Snippet Sensations project, in the order in which they are used (supplies and fabrics will vary depending upon the type of project you are going to create). Please read the General Instructions in Part II because those detailed instructions are given to help you choose the appropriate supplies for your individual project.

Design source. An image you use as a guide or for inspiration.

Foundation fabric. The base on which to build your project. The color of the foundation fabric is determined by background style.

Palette fabric. Fabric in all colors and prints needed to create your Snippet design.

Palette fabric

Fusible web. Use two-sided fusing web; approximately 1/2 yard for each square foot of the project.

Scissors. Must be sharp and comfortable.

Steam iron and ironing board.

Sewing machine and basic sewing supplies. Only necessary for projects with sewing.

Quilting supplies. Only necessary for quilted projects.

Framing supplies. Only necessary for framed projects.

Fusible web

Embellishments. Optional; includes charms, fabric pens, beads, and buttons.

The colorful Snippet Sensations fabric used in the headings and around the tip boxes was designed by Cindy for Springs. It is available at your favorite fabric shop.

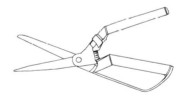

*Scissors
(Fiskars Softouch)*

Embellishment

Process Preview

Snippet projects are created by following a sequence of easy steps, which are discussed in detail in Part II. Here is a summary of the Snippet Sensations technique.

1. Choose a design. Design and inspiration sources are limitless!

2. Choose a foundation and background style that suits your design. The background style determines what to use as the foundation fabric. The fabric can be completely covered with snippets or panels, or partially exposed as part of the all-over design.

3. Collect the palette fabrics needed to create your design. Color, pattern, and texture are important considerations.

4. Gather ironing equipment and scissors.

5. Choose a fusible web and pre-fuse it to the wrong side of the palette fabric pieces.

6. Clean up the pre-fused palette fabrics by cutting around all of the edges to trim away loose threads, excess fusible web, and fabric areas without fusible web.

7. Determine the design depth and order of the snippet layers. The design elements will be placed onto the foundation in their order of depth, starting with the farthest elements and ending with the nearest.

8. Cut and create the Snippet project. If the project has a background, create this before the image.

9. Once finished, use an iron to permanently set the snippets in place. Review and critique your project from a distance before this final step. Trim the foundation to the desired size, or trim to center the motif.

10. Finish your project in any manner desired: frame it, turn into a quilt, or use it as a panel in a garment.

General Instructions   PART II

*T*here are several approaches to creating a Snippet project. This section provides what you need to make any of the beautiful projects in this book or a masterpiece of your own design. Please read Part II carefully.

Design Idea

Any image can be transformed into a Snippet project, from still life to abstract. Design ideas can come from any source; use a picture, draw a design, or use an image from your mind. Many of my designs have come from my own photography. I prefer working from a photograph, or picture, because I can study the shadows and colors. I also use the paintings of great master artists, like Van Gogh, for inspiration; study their use of color and brushstroke movement.

Awakening, 18" x 15", 1999, by Joyce R. Becker. When stress threatens to send Joyce "over the edge," her spirit finds peace, harmony, and renewal in her imaginary, impressionistic garden. Inspired by a Thomas Kinkade print and Claude Monet, she kept her color values low in contrast to evoke calmness and serenity. This quilt was exhibited at AQS in Paducah, KY, in 1999. It received an honorable mention at the Western Washington State Fair 1998 and received a blue ribbon at the Washington Evergreen Piecemakers' Quilt Show 1998. Joyce is the author of Nature's Patterns *(Quilt Digest Press).*

Glacier National Park, 28" x 24", 1999, by Judy Lundberg. Judy started this quilt in a Snippet class with Cindy in Rhode Island. Her inspiration was a photograph she had taken at Glacier National Park in Montana. Free-motion quilting with metallic and rayon threads completes the design.

Some types of designs are easier than others. Pictures with a single image, still life objects, or landscapes are "forgiving" subjects and easily translate into a Snippet project. Images such as portraits or animals are "less forgiving" because you have to pay more attention to detail.

Select design ideas that have a high color contrast in the different areas of the picture. If the sky, trees, and water are all a shade of teal, it will be difficult to distinguish between the different elements in the finished project.

Eventually, you will see Snippet design possibilities everywhere you look!

Beaverton, 17″ x 20″, 1997, by Linda Schaufele (1944–1998). Beaverton was Linda's mischievous, but adorable, cat. She certainly captured his luxurious fur and distinctive expression, as well as his favorite catnip-stuffed toy spider. This was only her second Snippet project; her artistic talent is quite evident.

Foundation Fabric and Background Style

The foundation fabric is the base upon which your Snippet project is built. Once you decide on the design idea, the next step is to decide upon the type of background style you would like to use. There are four types of background styles; they determine the type and color of fabric you will use for the foundation. Your foundation can be partly exposed as an essential part of the design, covered with panels, completely covered with snippets, or a combination thereof.

Partly Exposed Foundation

For this type of background, the foundation fabric shows through as a part of the entire design. For a three-dimensional effect, the exposed foundation should be the element that is the farthest away in the distance, for example the sky in a landscape scene.

Owl I, by Cindy Walter. This demonstrates an exposed foundation.

10

Foundation Covered With Panels

This style of background uses large pieces, or panels, of fabric to completely cover a white foundation. The panels create the background for a design image.

Owl II, *by Cindy Walter. This piece has a panel background.*

Foundation Covered With Snippets

This type of background uses small snippets of fabric to completely cover a white foundation, giving a wonderful impressionistic look. Covering the entire foundation with snippets uses more fabric, and takes extra time, but it is well worth the effort.

Owl III, *by Cindy Walter. The background of this piece is made up of snippets*

Foundation Combination

You can also combine the above background styles, or even sew pieces of fabric together, to create the foundation.

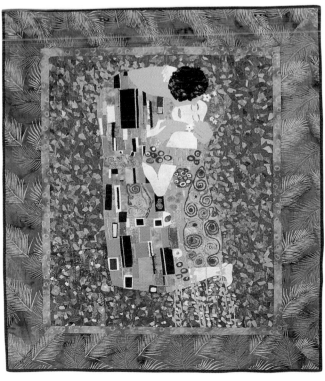

The Kiss II, *40″ x 47″, 1996, by Cindy Walter. The passion in Klimt's painting inspired me to create this Snippet project. The green foundation is exposed, but it is covered with random-shaped gold snippets, which lend the appearance of a snippet foundation. The couch, on which they are kneeling, and their gowns are made from large panels. This project is a true example of the Snippet technique, because it combines different foundation styles and both random-shaped and predetermined-shaped snippets.*

Types of Fabrics for Foundations

Any type of fabric will work for the foundation as long as it can be ironed. I prefer cotton, but I have created projects on velvet, linen, and silk. The foundation can be anything from white muslin, if you are going to cover it, to a beautiful hand-dyed silk, if you are going to leave it partly exposed.

The size of the foundation is completely up to you. Cut the foundation several inches wider and longer than the desired finished size; this will give you room to play.

Mainau Parrots, *23″ x 26″, 1999, by Cindy Walter. I wanted the parrots to stand out in the sunlight, with the dark forest receding behind them, so I used Diana Leone's bright fabrics from Northcott/Monarch to create the birds and put them on black velour. It is fun to use a variety of fabric types in your Snippet projects. (Before using a new type of fabric, test it to make sure it can be ironed for 15 seconds.) The veins on the leaves and flowers were created by free-motion quilting with Mettler metallic threads.*

Fabric for Snippets

I refer to these as the palette fabrics, because you are "painting" with snippets of these assorted fabric colors and textures. Projects usually take a small amount of a large variety of fabrics. Remember, Snippets means freedom... you may change the color or amount of each fabric at will.

Types of Fabrics

Fabric scrap bags are perfect for Snippet Sensations. Almost any type of fabric can be used for a Snippet project as long as you can iron it. Test fabrics in question before use by ironing them the instructed amount of time on the fusible web's packaging. Experiment with colors, textures, and prints of many different fabrics. Raw linen can add wonderful texture to leaves, or how about silk for flower petals? These fabrics can add texture that cotton can't. Several projects in this book use a combination of fabric types. Cottons are the easiest to use because, when setting the project, the heat of the iron evenly permeates the fusible web glue. Consider using a protective cloth when

*For her quilt, **Splendid**, Anne Anderson used hand-painted silk charmeuse (see page 49 for the full quilt).*

ironing delicate fabrics such as silk or satin, and keep in mind that you may have to iron thick fabrics like broadcloth longer than other lighter fabrics.

Fabric Prints

Fabrics of all prints can be used in a Snippet project. I avoid using solid fabrics because they tend to be "flat," but they do give a distinctive, crisp, defined look. Printed fabrics with multiple colors and values add incredible visual texture, much like a brushstroke of paint. You might be intimidated by printed fabrics, but I think you will like the impressionistic result they achieve. Printed monochromatic fabrics are my favorite choice because they stay in one color family, yet still add the texture of a print.

Color-on-color fabrics, designed by Diana Leone for Northcott/ Monarch, are easy to use because they stay in one color family.

Fun with Bugs, 28″ x 25″, 1996, by Sue Wilson. This project is a great gift for any child or bug collector. Make a wreath by scattering a variety of greens in a large circle and embellish it with bugs, butterflies, or any creature cut from printed fabric. To finish the project, top it with a wire-rimmed bow. Refer to Project 13, Rochelle's Wreath (on page 90) for wreath directions.

I am crazy about hand-dyed and batik fabrics; you will find them in many of my projects. Sometimes you can use the motifs that are printed right on the fabric as part of your project (for instance, you can put a butterfly on your flower bouquet by simply fussy cutting one right from themed butterfly fabric).

Amount of Fabric Needed

Closely examine your design source. Gather the fabrics for your palette and determine how much you need of each piece. The amount of each fabric you need depends upon the project size and the proportion of each color to the overall design. For example, a few snippets of red in a sunset would require only a small amount of fabric, perhaps one 2″ square piece. On the other hand, a large red barn would use several larger pieces of red, perhaps a variety of six pieces at 6″ x 6″, each. To be safe, pre-fuse a little more fabric than you think you will need.

Pre-wash Fabric

Several of the fusible webs currently on the market adhere better to pre-washed fabric than unwashed. As a rule, I pre-wash all of my fabrics in the washing machine when I bring them home. Do not use any soaps, rinses, or fabric softeners—you want to remove these chemicals, not add them.

Felis Concolor, 48″ x 40″, 1999, by Deborah Sylvester. Inspired by a photograph taken by Daniel L. Cox in the 1999 calendar "The Big Cats," Deborah cut more than 10,000 snippets of fabric to create this majestic cat. It was a finalist in the 1999 International Quilt Association's "Quilts, a Work of Beauty" and the 1999 Yokohama Quilt Week in Japan. This quilt was also featured at the Braddigins Arts and Craft Gallery, Hillsborough, NC.

Fusible Web

Fusible web (sometimes called webbing) is a sheet of web-like glue with release paper on one side, or both. When heat is applied, the web permanently adheres one fabric to another. This fabric-to-fabric bonding is done in two stages. The first bond occurs when the web is adhered to the assorted snippet fabrics (when pre-fusing palette fabrics). Once the snippets are in place, the second bonding occurs when snippets are fused to the foundation fabric. The web, depending upon the brand, is referred to in many ways, including iron-on adhesive, transfer web, appliqué webbing, iron-on fabric fusing web, and paper-backed fusible web.

Tip

Fusible web should not be confused with single-sided iron-on interfacing.

Fusible Web Characteristics

There are many brands of double-sided, paper-backed, fusible web on the market. Some of the brands you may be familiar with are Aleene's Fusible Web, Heat N Bond, and WonderUnder (in this book, I refer to these types of webs as "traditional"). One of the major differences among these products is the length of time the hot iron is left in place so that the web has time to bond the fabrics together. For this reason, I strongly recommend that you use only one type of web on any given project. Ten seconds of heat may securely bond one brand of web, but for another brand, this length of time could be either too much or inadequate.

There is a newer, revolutionary, fusible web on the market called Steam-A-Seam2. Both sides of the web are treated with a pressure sensitive adhesive, which means the fabric temporarily adheres to the web without ironing. Therefore, you pre-fuse without an iron; the web temporarily sticks with just the pressure of your hand. Because the web is pressure-sensitive on both sides, the "pre-fused" piece of fabric will also temporarily adhere to the foundation fabric. Once you are finished with the Snippet project, fuse with a hot steam iron to make the temporary hold permanent.

In the following chapters of this book, when I refer to fusible web, I will be referring to Steam-A-Seam2. **If you are using a different web, it is important to closely follow the directions that come with the brand you choose because each brand of web has specific instructions for the fusing process.**

To determine the amount of fusible web to buy, consider the finished size of your project. You will need approximately 1/2 yard of web for each square foot of the finished project.

Tip

Remember: To avoid disasters, use one brand of web per project and follow the manufacturer's directions.

To Use Steam-A-Seam2 Fusible Web

To pre-fuse palette fabrics to Steam-A-Seam2, pull off one of the paper liners to expose the web. Set the wrong sides of the palette fabrics on top of the web and gently press with your hand. Then, cut out the palette fabrics, trimming away any exposed web or fabric without web. Keep the second paper liner on until you are ready to use that piece of fabric. To remove the second paper liner, bend a corner toward the paper. The paper will stay bent and the fabric will spring back to place, making it easy to remove the paper liner.

To permanently set the project when it is complete, use a hot steam iron. Press each area for 15 seconds; lift up the iron and move it to the next area. Do not move the iron back and forth because you might disturb the placement of your snippets. Never under-iron with Steam-A-Seam2; iron for the full 15 seconds. Use an ironing cloth if your iron is dirty or if you are working with delicate fabrics such as silk or lamé.

To Use Other Brands of Fusible Web

To pre-fuse palette fabrics with a traditional web, **closely follow the directions that come with it**. In general, you will set the wrong side of the fabric on the web and iron for the instructed amount of seconds. Do not over iron! Then, cut out the palette fabrics, trimming away any exposed web or fabric without web. Keep the paper liner on until you are ready to use that piece of fabric. To remove the paper liner, bend a corner toward the paper. The paper will stay bent and the fabric will spring back to place, making it easy to remove the paper liner.

To permanently set the project when it is complete, use a hot iron. Press each area, for the instructed amount of seconds stated on the package directions, by lifting up the iron and moving it to the next area. Do not move the iron back and forth because you might disturb the placement of your snippets. Never over-iron with traditional webs because excessive heat will ruin the integrity of the glue. Use an ironing cloth if your iron is dirty or if you are working with delicate fabrics such as silk or lamé.

Scissors

You will need scissors for every project. I prefer Fiskars Softouch™ scissors because of the shape of their blades and their spring release, which prevents my hand from becoming tired. The Fiskars Micro Tip Softouch™ is smaller and is wonderful for cutting very tiny "precision" snippets. Your scissors must be sharp; otherwise you will get frayed nerves and have frayed edges on your snippets.

Rotary cutting equipment is very handy for cutting the foundation and border fabrics and for squaring up the edges of a completed project.

Alaskan Sunset, *26″ x 18″, 1997, by Cindy Walter. The beautiful fabric for this quilt was provided by Alaska Dyeworks. I made the project with rotary equipment using a special Olfa cutting wave blade to create the rippled effects of the sky and water. To create this effect, after pre-fusing the palette fabrics, pull off the web's remaining paper liner. Set the pre-fused fabrics glue side up on a large Omnigrid mat and just cut with the wave blade.*

Steam Iron and Ironing Board

You need a steam iron and ironing board for every project. Check the fusible web directions to see at what temperature to set the iron and whether or not to use steam. Steam-A-Seam2 fusible web requires a cotton setting and steam because the extra heat helps set the web, while some webs do not require steam. Also, keep your iron clean. If your hot iron touches the web, wipe it clean immediately to avoid ruining your project.

Because Steam-A-Seam2 is pressure sensitive and the snippets temporarily adhere to the foundation, you can pick the project up and move it to the ironing board when it is time to permanently set the project. When using other types of web, it is difficult to move the project without disturbing the snippets. In this case, I suggest using a makeshift ironing board made of cardboard. Cut a piece of cardboard (without creases) slightly larger than your foundation. Lay the foundation on the cardboard, create your Snippet project, and iron it right on the cardboard.

You Are Now Ready to Get Started

1. **Once you have a design idea,** you are ready to get started. Study the design idea to determine the best foundation and palette fabrics for your project.

2. **Select the foundation fabric** and cut it to the required size. Iron to remove wrinkles.

3. **Select and pre-fuse the palette fabrics.** Remember to read the web package's directions carefully and use only one type of web per project. When using Steam-A-Seam2, remove one of the paper liners and set the wrong side of the fabric on the web. Gently press with your hand. To pre-fuse with traditional web, use the heat of an iron to adhere the web to the wrong side of the palette fabrics (read package directions carefully).

4. **Clean up the palette fabrics** after pre-fusing them by trimming away frayed edges, excess web, or areas of fabric without web. Leave the paper liner on the back of the pre-fused fabrics until you are ready to use that piece. Important! Peel off the paper liner before cutting snippets!

5. **Lay the foundation fabric, right side up, on your workspace.**

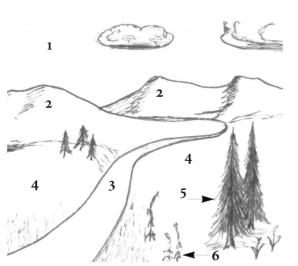

6. **Determine the working order.** Always start with the objects that are the farthest away and end with the objects that are closest, or on top. For instance, in a landscape, create the sky first and end with the small flowers on the ground closest to you. Occasionally, I cut pieces that are significant to the design and put them on the foundation. For instance, when making a flower bouquet, the stems are behind the vase and should be cut first, but for a guideline, I create the vase first and then cut the stems, tucking them behind the vase.

7. **Determine what shape to cut the snippets.** You have the freedom to choose the shapes of the snippets as well as where to place them. The individual projects will give you guidelines for cutting the assorted shapes of the snippets used in each area of that project. Don't forget, the concept behind Snippets is *freedom*. Do as little pre-drawing or worrying as possible. For instance, to make a stem, just cut a long, sweeping piece of green—it's that easy. Or, to make a lilac, just cut random semi-round or oval-shaped snippets and let them fall, creating a purple mound. This might sound intimidating and not specific enough, but once you try it, you will find it is easy and accurate—and refreshing!

8. **Cut the snippets right over the foundation, with the tips of the scissors actually touching the foundation.** Most of the snippets will fall right in place (and with glue side down). Important! Remember to take the paper off before cutting snippets (even the best of us have made this mistake)! Check to make sure all snippets are glue side down, because they can flip over while cutting. If you are using a traditional web, iron the project in stages (after two or three layers of snippets) to prevent them from shifting. For Steam-A-Seam2, use hand pressure to temporarily adhere the snippets to the background.

9. **During the creation of your Snippet project, take the time to stand back** about 10 feet from your project at least once or twice, to get a long-range view of the image that is emerging. You can fix areas by repositioning snippets or by adding more. Sometimes it is even helpful to leave your project overnight and approach it again when you are refreshed in the morning. Don't forget, you always have complete freedom to add new snippets to your foundation fabric.

10. **Set the snippets permanently.** To finish, make sure all of the snippets are glue side down. Iron the entire piece according to the fusible web's package instructions to permanently set the snippets in place. With Steam-A-Seam2, fuse with a hot steam iron for a full 15 seconds in each area.

11. **If you are creating a fabric art project, determine whether to quilt or frame your project. If you are creating a wearable, now is the time to turn the project into the garment.** For further information on framing and quilting, see Part III.

Flower Bouquet, *24″ x 28″, 1999, by Cindy Walter. This simple, yet elegant, quilt features a wide range of beautiful summer flowers created with random-shaped snippets. We have included step-by-step directions and photographs so you can create a flower bouquet like the one shown here. This easy project will familiarize you with cutting random and specifically shaped snippets.*

Project Demonstration

*F*lower *B*ouquet

This project demonstration was designed to give you further instructions on how to cut snippets. Even if you are not interested in making a flower bouquet, read this section to gain a thorough understanding of the process.

1. Collect the supplies.

Foundation fabric
White . . . . .16″ x 20″
Vase fabric
Purple . . . . .8″ x 6″
Foliage fabric
Green . . . . .10″ x 12″
Flower fabrics . .Variety 6″ x 6″ (each)
(7 or 8 different colors, including
yellow, purple, and orange)
Steam-A-Seam2 . . . . .1 yd.
Sharp scissors
Ironing equipment
Border fabric . . . . 1/4 yd.
Floral blue border fabric . . . .1/2 yd.
Binding fabric . . . . .1/8 yd.
Batting . . . . 26″ x 30″
Backing fabric . . . . 26″ x 30″
Machine quilting supplies

2. Pre-fuse the palette fabrics by removing one of Steam-A-Seam2's paper liners and setting the fabrics on the web.

3. Clean up the fabrics by trimming around each piece, slightly into the fabric to remove any extra threads, exposed web, and fabric without web.

4. Cut the foundation to the correct size and iron, if needed. Once your fabrics are pre-fused and cleaned-up, you are ready to start.

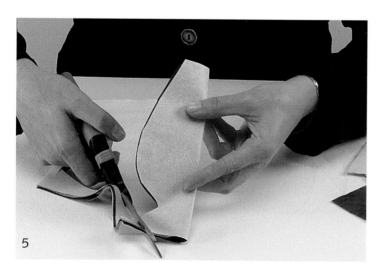

5. Start by creating the vase. Fold the pre-fused vase fabric in half lengthwise and cut a half vase shape from the non-fold side. Remove the remaining paper liner and put the vase in place, about 2˝ from the bottom of the foundation.

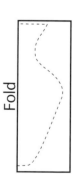

Fold

6. Remove the paper liner from the back of the green fabric and cut long, sweeping pieces to create greenery.

7. Create a base for the flowers with as much greenery as possible. Mix and match greens, if desired. The leaves and ferns do not need to be connected; some can be long and tucked into the vase, while others can be short and fill in the outer areas. For a three-dimensional effect, you can go back later and add a few leaves on top of the flowers.

8. Now, start to cut the flowers. Cut random-shaped pieces from the purple fabric to create lilacs. Remember to use the tip of the scissors and to cut right on the foundation. Don't fret over the shapes in the lilacs—make them completely random. Make about five lilacs.

9. For the next flower, a daisy, cut random-shaped spears from the yellow fabric and place them in a circle. Cut a circle from your darkest fabric to add to the center of the daisies. Make about three daisies.

10. With the remaining yellow fabric, create goldenrods by cutting random shapes and placing them in sweeping arches to add color to the project.

11. To create a tulip, cut a circle, about 2″ in diameter, from orange fabric, two quarter "moons" off each side of the circle, and three spears from the remaining center piece. Place the three spears upright together and then the two quarter moons on either side. Make as many tulips as desired. Scatter them throughout the bouquet.

12. Spider mums are large, delicate flowers. Place one or two of them wherever you need color. Make large spider mums by cutting sweeping, thin pieces from a large oval. Place about five arches on both sides of the mum, with a smaller one on the top and bottom.

13. If desired, fussy cut flowers from floral fabric as a final touch. If I am using a floral fabric as the border, I often scatter a few of the flowers from the border fabric throughout the bouquet to pull all of the colors together.

14. Once you are finished with your project, check to make sure all of the snippets are glue side down. View the project from a distance. Are the colors dispersed well? Are you happy with the overall effect?

13

15. Set the project by pressing for 15 seconds in each area. Press by picking the iron up and placing it in the next area. Do no "iron" back and forth because you could disturb the small snippets.

15

16. It is now time to finish the top as a quilt. Add borders like the quilt example on page 20 (refer to page 28 for detailed instructions). Cut two strips from the blue border fabric, each 1-1/2″ x 20″. Sew these to the long sides of the top and iron the seams away from the foundation. Cut two more blue strips, each 1-1/2″ x 18″. Sew these to the top and bottom of the top and iron the seams away from the foundation. Cut two strips from the floral fabric, each 3-1/2″ x 22″. Sew these to the sides of the top and iron the seams away from the foundation. Cut two more strips from the floral fabric, each 3-1/2″ x 24″. Sew these to the top and bottom of the top and iron the seams away from the foundation. You are now ready to finishing your quilt (see Part III, beginning on page 26, to learn how to layer, machine quilt, and bind your project).

16

Now is the time to decide how you will finish your Snippet project. Would you like to frame it like a piece of artwork, use it as part of a garment, or turn it into a quilted wall hanging?

Framed

If you would like to frame your Snippet project, take it to your local framing shop for advice. Do not trim off the extra foundation fabric until the framer determines whether the extra fabric is needed for the framing process. Use glass or Plexiglas to prevent dust from collecting on your project. Once framed, you truly have a piece of Fabric Art!

Dream Patio, 11″ x 14″, 1999, by Debra Schuh. The wonderful, multicolored ground fabric is the exposed foundation on which Debra constructed the project. She drew the chair on the fusible web's paper liner, as in an appliqué pattern, and then created the rest of the project with tiny snippets.

Garments

Create snippets right on a pre-made garment, or create a garment from scratch. When designing a garment from scratch, create each panel separately and sew them together after the Snippet and quilting processes.

Christmas Sweatshirt, *1998, by Mindy Draper. Mindy made this sweatshirt for her grandmother (Cindy's aunt), Connie Draper, as a Christmas present. What a great idea! You can embellish any pre-made washable or dry-cleanable garment with snippets. Using a seam, or hidden hem area, test to make sure you are able to iron the fabric for 15 seconds.*

Quilted

Turning your Snippet masterpiece into a small quilt or quilted wall hanging is a great way to finish your project. If you are experienced in this area, quilt your project as desired. If you need a helping hand, follow along with the rest of this section through which you will learn how to add borders, layer the quilt, machine quilt, and bind.

Tip

Fusible web also works on paper or cardboard. Add snippets to greeting cards for home decorating applications.

Mother's Day Card, 4-1/4″ x 5-1/2″, 1998, by Koni Jeremica. This is a Snippet greeting card made on construction paper. Koni helped the girls in her daughters' Girl Scout troop make similar cards for their mothers. What a great project for any season or holiday! Here, fabric is adhered to paper. You can use construction paper or pre-made blank stationery, but be sure to test the paper for the appropriate ironing time (approximately 5 seconds).

You can make spectacular holiday cards that are quick and easy—and that your family and friends will cherish.

Turn Your Project into a Quilt

There are several steps to complete before your project is ready to quilt, such as trimming the foundation to the correct size, adding borders, layering it with the batting and backing, and basting the three layers together. Snippet projects lend themselves to machine quilting, because it is difficult to hand quilt through fusible web.

Once your project is finished and ironed to permanently set the fusible web, check to make sure the motif is centered correctly on the foundation and that the edges are straight. Use the guidelines on your rotary mat and your rotary equipment to square up your project or center the motif if necessary.

Borders

Borders are a project's final framework. Depending upon the look you are trying to achieve, you may decide upon no border at all, or select from an endless number of them. For instance, some contemporary types of quilts do not have a border, like Fragrant Memories (on the cover and page 42). On the other hand, Snippet projects are a perfect base to add numerous or creative borders. There is no "right or wrong" way when it comes to choosing borders; it is completely your choice. I suggest laying the proposed border fabrics around the Snippet project, standing back, and auditioning them. Do they help create the look you desire by adding to the all-over image or do they subtract from it? The color of the border will dominate the quilt, so choose colors and fabrics you want to feature.

Sewing on Borders

If you are a beginner, I suggest using block-style borders. Here is how to measure, cut, and sew them on:

1. Measure the two longest sides of the foundation (these measurements should be the same). Cut two border strips this length by the desired border width.

2. Using a 1/4″ seam allowance, sew the border strips onto the long edges of the foundation. Iron the seams away from the foundation.

3. Measure the two remaining sides, including the attached borders. Cut two border strips this length by the desired border width.

4. Using a 1/4″ seam allowance, sew the border strips to the remaining sides. Iron the seams away from the foundation.

5. If you want two or three layers of borders, simply repeat the above process.

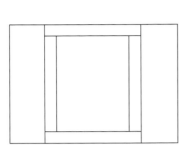
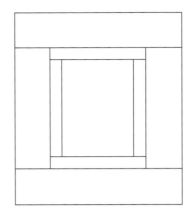

When adding borders to my Snippet projects, I often use a small "framing" border on the inside with a wider main border on the outside. This gives the appearance that the project has been framed with a double mat. Choose a bold fabric for the framing border and follow the procedure above, cutting the strips 1-1/2″ wide. Completely sew on the framing border, and then start again, following the procedure above to add the main border.

Graceful Ivy, 26″ x 29″, 1998, by Cindy Walter. The soft, pastel fabrics from Fabrics To Dye For give this quilt a calming effect. To make this project, I followed the directions for the step-by-step flower bouquet (on page 21) with two exceptions: I cut a pitcher by first drawing it on the fusible web paper, and then I cut the leaves in an irregular ivy shape.

Backing Fabric

The color and design of the quilt back should complement and enhance the work on the quilt's top. The backing fabric should also match or blend in with the bobbin thread. I choose the bobbin thread before choosing the backing fabric. Even when a sewing machine's tension is perfect, you will still see a tiny dot of bobbin thread on the top of the quilt, just as you see a tiny dot of top thread on the back. Don't use white bobbin thread if the top of your quilt is made up of primarily dark colors. For a dark-colored top, use dark bobbin thread with a dark backing fabric that matches the colors of the quilt top. A tip is to use a printed backing fabric; this allows you a larger choice of bobbin thread colors and hides mistakes. Cut the backing fabric at least 1˝ larger all around than the finished Snippet quilt top in case the fabric shifts slightly during quilting.

Batting

Batting is the soft filler that is layered, or sandwiched, between the quilt top and backing to add loft. For machine quilting, I suggest using cotton batting. It has a wonderful quality of "holding the layers together" while quilting, which is important to help prevent shifting and puckers. Ask your local shop for the best quality cotton batting it carries—don't skimp on cost!

There are several good battings on the market. I use Warm n' Natural Cotton for most of my Snippet projects because they are designed to be wall hangings; this needle-punched cotton helps my quilts hang flat and square. For a baby quilt, you might try a more drapable type of batting like Hobbs Heirloom cotton. Regardless of which type you choose, cut the batting at least 1˝ larger all around than the finished Snippet quilt top.

There is no need to pre-wash any of the battings currently on the market. In the past several years, the major manufacturers have changed how they make batting; not only are they pre-washing the cotton batting for you, they are also removing the seeds and other natural fibers to make the batting easier to work with.

Layer and Baste the Quilt

The quilt "sandwich" is made up of the top, batting, and backing fabric. To layer a project, lay the backing fabric right side down on your work surface (tape if necessary). Center the batting on top of the backing, and then center the quilt top, right side up, on top of the batting.

Because of the fusible web layers, the best method to baste a Snippet quilt is either with safety pins or with a fabric spray adhesive. Traditional thread basting or the use of a "tagging" gun are both difficult because of the fusible web's thickness.

Safety Pin Basting

To safety pin baste,

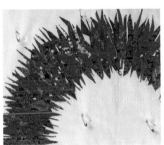

1. Lay the backing fabric right side down on a large table or tile floor. Tape the fabric to the floor or table on all four sides.
2. Center the batting over the backing fabric; carefully smooth any wrinkles.
3. Center the quilt top, right side up, on the batting. Carefully smooth any wrinkles, working from the center outward, being careful not to stretch the quilt top out of shape.
4. Beginning in the center and working your way out to the edges, slide a safety pin (nickel or brass-plated, size 1 or 2) though all three layers and back up to the top every 3″ to 4″.
5. Do not try to close the safety pins as you go because you might disturb the project. Once all of the safety pins are in, go back and close them.

(Note: When quilting, remove the safety pins before you reach them.)

Fabric Spray Adhesives

Fabric spray adhesives temporarily hold the quilt layers together while quilting. KK 2200, 505, and Dritz are all good brands, and I find them to be fast and efficient when working with small quilts. For larger quilts (i.e. bed-size), I use the safety pin basting method because I find it difficult to properly sandwich larger quilts with the spray adhesive. I do not recommend using any chemicals on heirloom-quality quilts.

To use spray adhesive,
1. Lay the backing fabric right side down on a large table or tile floor. Tape the backing fabric to the floor or table on all four sides.
2. Spray the backing fabric with a light, even mist of the spray adhesive.
3. Center the batting over the backing; carefully smooth any wrinkles.
4. Spray the batting with a light, even mist of spray adhesive.
5. Center the quilt top, right side up, over the batting; carefully smooth any wrinkles.

Machine Quilting

Machine quilting is a fast and efficient way to finish your Snippet project. Consider the quilting lines to be final brushstrokes on your canvas. Analyze the project to determine where you will place the quilting stitches and what colors of thread to use.

Consider quilting lines to be your final brushstrokes.

Supplies for Machine Quilting

❊ Sewing machine in good working order with a large working surface

❊ Walking foot (for straight line quilting and attaching the binding)

❊ Free-motion darning foot (for free-motion quilting)

❊ Topstitch or denim needle, size 90

❊ Cotton machine-quilting thread (for top and bobbin)

❊ Other decorative threads (optional)

❊ Quilter's gloves or machine-quilting hoop (optional)

After years of practice, I have developed tricks to help make my long hours spent at the sewing machine enjoyable:

• If you are in the market to buy a darning foot, buy a spring darner. It pushes the fabric downward as the needle comes up which is helpful in preventing threads from breaking.

• If your needle is too thin, as with a universal or metallic needle, it will not poke a large enough hole for the thread to easily come back up through all of the layers. Use a bigger, stronger needle called a topstitch needle (size 90); it has a sharp point and a fat shaft. It also has a very large eye suitable for decorative threads and ease of threading. If you can't find a topstitch needle, I recommend a denim needle (size 90) because it also has a sharp point and a fat shaft. If your threads break for no apparent reason while quilting, change your needle; a dull needle or one with a burr on the end can cause problems. Needles are inexpensive; always start a new project with a new needle.

- **This is one of the most important tips I can give you.** Use machine-quilting thread in the bobbin and on top of the machine (not hand-quilting thread). Strong machine-quilting thread can tolerate the stress of machine quilting and also of going in and out of many layers of fabric, fusible web, and batting. Even though we have always been taught to use bobbin thread, or match the weight of the top thread to the bobbin, I now only use machine-quilting thread in the bobbin. Some of the brands of machine-quilting thread I like to use include Mettler, Signature, and Coats & Clark. When using machine-quilting thread in the bobbin, it is easier to experiment with other types of threads on the top.

- Use quilter's gloves to eliminate stress on your arms and shoulders. They grip the quilt, making it easier to move.

- I always keep a practice "sandwich" nearby to check my machine's tension before starting a new project or changing thread types.

Straight-line Quilting

I use very little straight-line quilting on Snippet projects, because I prefer free-motion quilting. Straight-line quilting is used for quilting in the ditch or seams, echoing around patchwork, or crosshatching (grid) the entire quilt. It can also be used to establish sections of a quilt. When free-motion quilting, a large quilt can easily get stretched out of shape; to prevent this, I use my walking foot and straight-line quilting to establish areas and then free-motion in sections. This is especially helpful on a quilt that has gridded areas but also areas where you want to free-motion quilt, such as an Attic Window quilt.

1. Set the machine to normal straight sewing.
2. Use cotton quilting thread in the bobbin and on top and a larger needle, such as a topstitch (90).
3. Place a walking foot on the machine.
4. Work from the center out to the edges. Quilt several horizontal and vertical lines to create sections before quilting the remaining lines.
5. Quilt enough to hold the quilt securely together and to the specifications of the batting (per its package). Some cotton battings require a minimum of quilting every 3″, while others only need to be quilted every 10″.

Free-motion Machine Quilting

This is the type of machine quilting I use on my Snippet projects. Use this type of machine quilting to quilt movement into your project. Follow the design of your quilt, or create additional designs with the thread. I consider the quilting lines to be the final brushstrokes on my projects.

1. Set the machine to normal straight sewing. If you have a needle down position on your machine, use it. The needle will stay in the quilt, holding it in place if you have to stop to change directions or remove a basting pin.

2. Use cotton quilting thread in the bobbin and on top and a larger needle, such as a topstitch (90). Wind enough bobbins to get you through your entire project.

3. Place a darning foot on the machine and lower the feet dogs.

4. You will be quilting in all directions, without turning the quilt, by guiding it with your hands. The stitch length will be determined by how fast you move your hands and how fast the machine is running. The secret is to run the machine semi-fast (80 percent of maximum speed) and move your hands slowly, at a steady pace. Because you are moving your hands slowly, you have time to think ahead as to what direction to go to next. Learn the correct rhythm and your stitches will be an even length. Most students make the mistake of running the machine too slowly, which results in uneven stitches.

5. Keep your hands spread out on each side of the needle, guiding the quilt and holding it to prevent puckers. Quilt the area between your hands. Stop the machine and move your hands in front of the needle and then quilt the next area.

6. Start in the middle of each project and rotate outward; this may mean changing the color of your thread several times. Do not skip over areas to leave for later because you will end up with a pucker on the back. Work slowly and do not stretch the quilt out of shape. Remove basting pins, or any types of pins, before you reach them.

7. Remember to use the quilting lines to "quilt in the motion." To help the quilt lie flat, use about the same amount of quilting lines throughout the project. Excess quilting in one area and not enough in another can cause puckers. Quilt enough to hold the quilt securely together and to the specifications of the batting (per its package). Some cotton battings require a minimum of quilting every 3″, while others only need to be quilted every 10″.

Quilting the Motion

Practice free-motion quilting first on a sandwich (fabric, batting, and backing fabric) before quilting your project. These are the free-motion patterns I use most often; practice them on a large "sandwich."

Painting With Thread. Use the thread to paint the motion of your project. For instance, quilt waves in the water or clouds in the sky. Outline images or use the thread to paint part of the image such as the veins on a leaf.

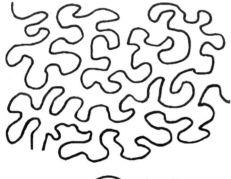

Stipple. A meandering motion, constantly turning without crossing over itself, as in the edges of puzzle pieces. This is a perfect stitch to fill in blank areas. Stipple curves can be small to very large. If you start off with a small, tight stipple curve, remember you need to continue that amount of quilting throughout the quilt in order for it to hang flat.

Ziggle. A meandering motion similar to stippling, but easier. Allow yourself to cross over the previous quilting lines. This is a perfect, whimsical stitch to fill in blank areas.

Angular stipple. A meandering motion, constantly turning and creating angles of all degrees, without crossing over itself. It is similar to stipple quilting but with angles instead of curves. This is a great stitch to fill in black areas on a masculine, or modern art, type of project.

Swirls, features, and hearts. Quilt any type of motif to enhance your quilt. All of these patterns are easy with a small bit of practice.

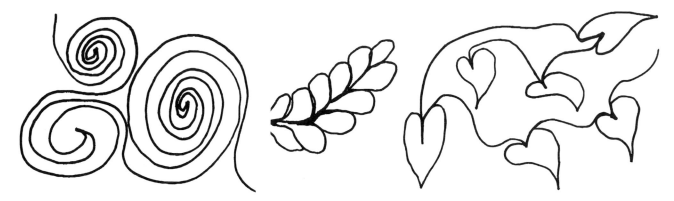

Secret Messages. Learn to write in cursive with your sewing machine. Write secret messages throughout your project. You can even sign your name in this manner!

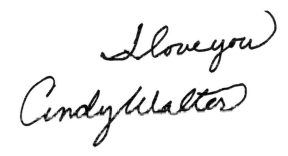

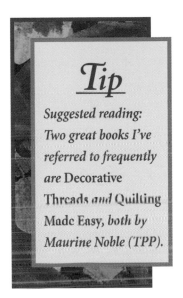

Tip

Suggested reading: Two great books I've referred to frequently are Decorative Threads *and* Quilting Made Easy, *both by* Maurine Noble (TPP).

Once you get comfortable with the rhythm of free-motion quilting, there is no end to the type of quilting lines you can create. Use your thread as a part of the all-over design. Remember to have about the same amount of quilting throughout the quilt to help it hang flat.

Embellishments

You can personalize your Snippet creation with a wide variety of embellishments, including threads, machine embroidery, couched-on yarns, or glued-on charms of your choice.

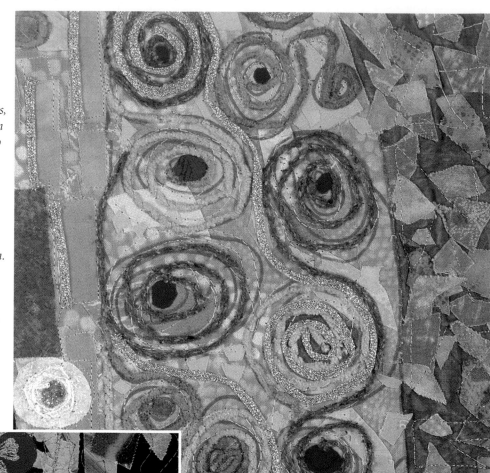

*An example of couched-on yarn from **The Kiss II** (see page 11 for the full quilt). Couching is an easy, fun way to embellish. Add yarns, braids, ribbons, or even thin strands of beads or pearls to your quilt. Attach the yarn (or other material) by zigzagging over it, securing it in place. You can use a clear monofilament thread or a highly contrasting colored thread over the yarn. If you have one, use a braiding or couching foot, although a regular zigzag foot will also work.*

*These machine-embroidered flowers (using my Husqvarna Viking Designer machine) on **Fragrant Memories** give the quilt another dimension (see page 42 for the full quilt). Machine embroider images on the quilt top, after setting snippets, but before layering the sandwich. If you embroider on just the top (and not the batting and backing), you will keep your quilt back free of the excess embroidery threads.*

*I thread-painted veins on the quilt **Mainau Parrots** (see page 12 for the full quilt).*

Binding

The binding is the edging sewn to the outer edges of the quilt to encase and finish the edge. I consider my binding to be the final border or frame of color. If your Snippet quilt has straight edges, cut the binding on the straight of the grain to make the edges of the quilt as straight as possible. If your quilt has curved edges, cut the binding strips on the diagonal. I use a single-fold binding on wall quilts rather than a double-fold. Because most Snippet quilts have straight edges, these instructions are for straight-cut single-fold binding.

1. Make the binding strips by cutting parallel strips of fabric 1-1/2″ wide with rotary equipment. Piece the strips together into one long, continuous strip. The length should match the project's perimeter, plus 6″.

2. Use a walking foot (dual feed foot) or a regular foot to sew the binding to the quilt's edge. Sew 3/8″ in from the raw edges.

3. With right sides together, align the raw edges of the binding with the front side of the quilt, beginning about 10″ from a corner. Fold the end of the binding downward at an angle.

5. Stop stitching 3/8″ from the corner and backstitch. Lift the needle out of the fabric (this is important). Pull the quilt a few inches away from the machine to loosen the threads.

6. Turn the quilt one quarter counterclockwise.

7. Fold the binding straight up (forming a 45° angle).

8. Fold the binding down over the angle, keeping the top folded edge even with the top of the quilt. Beginning at the top edge, sew the seam. Repeat the miter step at the corners.

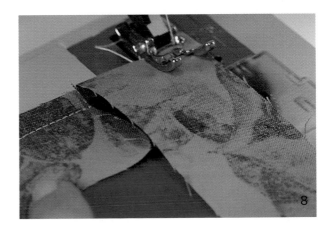

9. When you reach the end, overlap the binding about an inch, placing the end over the folded beginning edge.

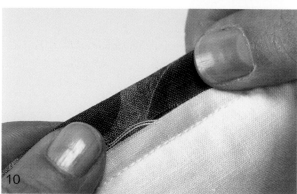

10. Working on the backside of the quilt and starting on a side, fold one quarter of the binding around to the back. Fold it one more time onto the back of the quilt.

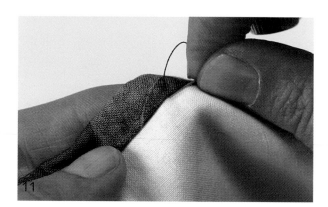

11. Hand-stitch the folded edge to the quilt back using a blind hemstitch with thread that matches the binding.

12. Tuck in the corners, forming a miter on the front and back.

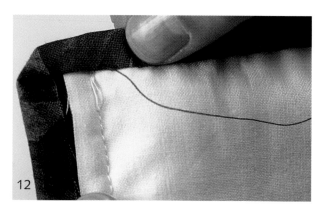

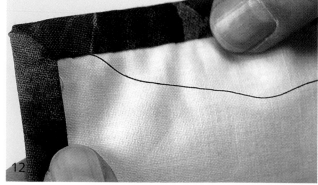

Labeling, Hanging, and Cleaning

Labeling

It is important for you to document your work. One easy way to do this is to make a fabric label. There are also decorative pre-made labels available at your local quilt shop. For either of these label types, write your name, address, and important information on the fabric with a waterproof pen, then stitch it to the back of your quilt. I use a permanent fabric pen to sign the front of my work with my initials and the year I made it.

Jeanne Coverdale, of Block Party Studios, Inc., made this custom label for me.

Hanging a Quilt

Sew a sleeve, rod pocket, or casing to the quilt's top back edge. Cut a 9″ wide strip from the same fabric as the backing. Piece strips if needed so the sleeve equals the exact width of the quilt's top edge. Seam the strip lengthwise to create a casing. Hand-sew both sides of the casing to the quilt, placing it 1/2″ from the top back edge. Use either a flat 1/4″ x 1-1/2″ board or a thin 1/2″ dowel to hang the quilt.

Cleaning

To clean your Snippet quilt, use a phosphorus-free soap, because detergents have harsh chemicals that may destroy the quilt; I recommend Orvus paste. Use one or two capfuls in the washing machine set on a gentle cycle. Lightly spin to remove excess water. I wash my Snippet projects in the bathtub just as with an heirloom quilt. Dry flat.

PART IV

Gallery of Snippet Quilts and Art

Fragrant Memories, *44-1/2″ x 33-1/2″, 1998, by Cindy Walter. I made this quilt for the invitational Quilts In Bloom art quilt show at the gallery of the Mainau Castle in Konstance, Germany. Starting with a large piece of black fabric, I added leaves and flowers of all types with bright fabric designed by Diana Leone. Before layering the quilt with the batting and backing, I added machine-embroidered flowers. The flower patterns came with my Husqvarna Viking sewing/embroidery machine. For the free-style machine quilting, I used a variety of Mettler machine-quilting threads.*

The Guardian, 65″ x 57″, 1999, by Deborah Sylvester. Deborah, who is an avid Snippet fan, teaches the technique in several quilt shops. This project was inspired by a print entitled "On this day...," by Lionel Talaro. The vivid fabrics are perfect for this project, which was featured at the Braddigins Arts and Craft Gallery, Hillsborough, NC.

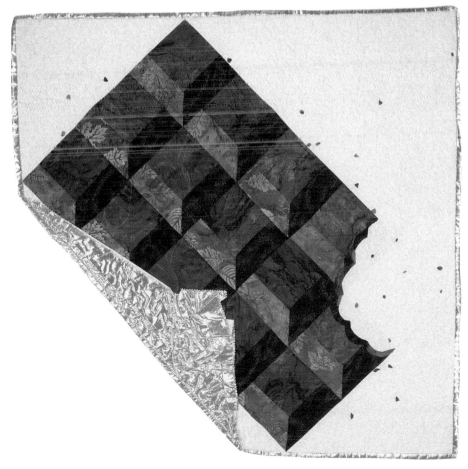

Who Needs P.M.S. to Eat Chocolate?, 38″ x 52″, 1998, by Deborah Sylvester. Deborah's inspiration to make this great quilt originated from a pregnant friend who couldn't get enough chocolate. She created the silver snippet wrapping with silver lamé. The center of the quilt is made from 13 pieced Attic Window blocks set on point. The quilt is featured in Attic Windows: Quilts With a View, by Diana Leone and Cindy Walter (Krause Publications) and hung at the Braddigins Arts and Craft Gallery, Hillsborough, NC.

Ladies Coming to Water, *1999, by Marvelyn Samuelson. As an artist, Marvelyn always had the desire to see if it were possible to paint with fabric. The Snippet technique gave her the opportunity to create an impression of the Southwest on a wearable. The jacket represents the countryside, and Native American cultures, of New Mexico. It's made up of different types, and colors, of silks. She created the Snippet image first and then machine quilted each jacket panel before piecing them together. She used WonderUnder as the fusing web, applying it to the silk before cutting the silk into hundreds of 1/2" squares and then layering them to achieve the desired effect. Great idea! The machine-quilting thread is Mylar, which adds a slight shimmer. The jacket has been displayed at several shows, including the Fiesta en Santa Fe Wearable Art Conference and Marin County Needlecraft Festival.*

44

***Berek at Koi Pond**, 30-1/2″ x 34-1/2″, 1999, by Tonya Littmann. In 1996, Tonya took a photo of her then 3-year-old son feeding the goldfish in their pond. She knew it was a great subject for a quilt but didn't know how to attempt it until Cindy introduced her to the Snippet technique. The quilt won a blue ribbon at the Dallas Quilt Celebration 2000, and, as the only fiber art piece in a show of paintings and sculptures, it was voted People's Choice at the North Texas Area Art League Show.*

Coastal Scene, 16″ x 19-1/2″, 1999, by Debra Schuh. Debra placed a panel of blue fabric (for the sky) on a foundation of white cotton. She used tweezers to place most of the small snippets. What a great use of color!

A Kiss on the River Dee, 12-1/2" x 17", 1999, by Deborah Mouser. Shortly after they were first married, Deborah and her husband kissed on this bridge in Scotland. Thread painting adds the final embellishment to this quilt.

New Mexico Visions, 30″ x 30″, 1999, by Melinda Lowy. Melinda's quilting guild held a "fabric challenge" in which the members had to use orange and purple plaid fabric. Having just visited the Southwest with her husband, she decided to make a project in memory of that trip. Unfortunately, Melinda missed the deadline for the guild's challenge, but all was not lost because she created this beautiful quilt!

Muir Woods, 14″ x 13-1/2″, 1999, by Judy Humphrey. While visiting Muir Woods in California, Judy thought it would be interesting to create a Snippet project with this scene of a pathway leading into the woods. The final embellishment of thread-painted trees really brings the scene to life.

Nature Lover's Dream, 40″ x 60″, 1998, by Kristine Calney. This quilt evolved from Kristine's desire to use the "Wildlife" embroidery card from her Janome Memorycraft 9000 sewing machine. She envisioned a circle of life with water as the center. The earth-toned fabrics help the natural environments flow into each other and surround each animal. It won a second place ribbon, and a special community award, at the 1998 Washington State Quilters Show.

Koalas, 13″ x 13″, 2000, by Tina Rathbone. A photo in a San Diego Zoo publication inspired Tina to create this quilt, which depicts a mother's protecting, maternal love for her baby. Tina's hand-dyed green and purple fabrics were the perfect choices for this project.

Sun Dancer, 50″ x 40″, 1998, by Deborah Sylvester and Cindy Walter. While Deborah was taking a class from Cindy at the International Quilt Festival in Houston, TX, she immediately became hooked on the Snippet technique. The inspiration for this quilt came from the painting "A Study for the Dancer in Red," by Arthello Beck Jr. After Deborah was finished with the Snippet portion of the project, Cindy machine quilted it and added the yarn embellishment. The machine quilting lines add movement to the quilt. Sun Dancer was a finalist in both the 1999 Mid-Atlantic Quilt Festival and the 1999 International Quilt Association's "Quilts, a World of Beauty" and was featured at the Braddigins Arts and Craft Gallery, Hillsborough, NC.

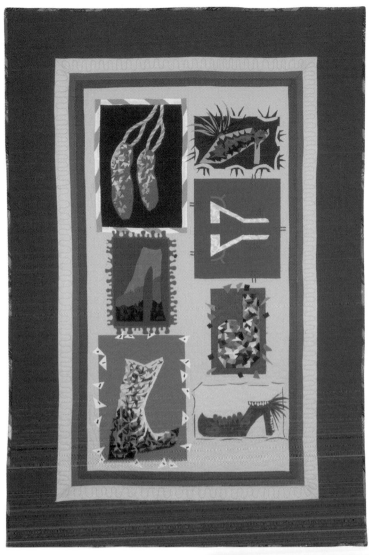

Shoes, 50″ x 70″, 1997, by Brielyn R. Doheny. Brielyn loves shoes and used this project to design her own fantasy collection! She fused the shoes onto individual blocks of fabrics and then fused each block onto the background which already had a border sewn around the edges. As the final touch, she fused borders around each shoe block. She got carried away with this quilt and enjoyed every minute of the creation process.

Splendid, 16″ x 20″, 2000, by Anne Anderson. Anne hand-painted the silk charmeuse used in this project. She is a fabric artist by trade, and painted silk is her specialty. The dyed silk results in luscious colors; she painted swatches of silk exactly the colors she needed for this brilliant red rose. (View Anne's silk art at www.anneanderson.com.)

The Three Queens (You Didn't Think the Wise Guys Remembered Gifts All by Themselves!) 20-1/2″ x 25″ unframed, 1996, by Meryl Ann Butler and Wendy Bush Hackney. This project was created with a combination of the Snippet technique, Holographic Prismatic Foil, and colored pencils. Meryl and Wendy sketched their design idea on tracing paper and made appliqué patterns for the main body parts of the queens, then added snippets over the appliqué pieces. They took turns creating the faces using Prismacolor pencils on the cotton fabric. The three gifts were made with Holographic Prismatic Foil. The piece is framed as a piece of fabric artwork.

West Coast of New Zealand, 23″ x 17″, 1999, by Simon Lee Johnson. Simon made this abstract picture of New Zealand's west coast with hand-dyed fabrics. The random machine quilting with variegated thread and the fabric colors make the landscape come to life.

Bluebonnets, 25-1/2″ x 31-1/2″, 1999, by Terri E. Vogds. Terri made this beautiful quilt from a photograph she took of her daughter Kelsie. Leftover scraps of fabric from the dress Kelsie wore in the photo were used to create the dress in the quilt. The bluebonnets and leaves are folded to create a three-dimensional effect. The thread-painted butterflies, a caterpillar, and a ladybug (Kelsie's nickname) add the final touches. Bluebonnets won a first place blue ribbon at the Mesquite Quilt Show in Texas.

Summer Fairie, 28″ x 30″, 2000, by Shannon Grant. Dragonflies escort this lovely fairy as she sprinkles fairy dust on the flowers. Shannon, an artist in her own right, is often inspired by the 1920's artist Cicely Mary Barker. She cut the dragonflies directly from printed fabric. The piece's mystical effect is achieved by machine quilting with metallic thread while the glued-on iridescent beads add sparkle to the fairy dust.

Salmon Run, 14″ x 14″, 2000, by Susan Smith and Cindy Walter. Cindy wanted to take an appliqué pattern and embellish it with snippets. She chose a pattern called Salmon Run (#NWS2) from Susan's company, Yellow Brick Road. After Susan made the quilt top according to the pattern's directions, Cindy added the snippets of Fabrics to Dye For fabrics and machine quilted the project. The Salmon Run pattern is part of a series of Northwest-inspired quilt blocks, commemorating the annual return of Salmon from the sea to the fresh water streams where they were born. The salmon are considered sacred to the Native American tribes of the Pacific Northwest and continue to be an important part of the culture and economy. Take an appliqué pattern of your choice and embellish it with additional fabrics of snippets to create a masterpiece of your own.

Dawn Of Remembrance: Egyptian Mysteries Unveiled, 1998, by Meryl Ann Butler with Wendy Bush Hackney. Meryl Ann created this incredible 13-piece ensemble by invitation for the 1998–1999 International Fairfield Fashion Show, the most prestigious designer's invitational wearable art fashion show in the world. The back panel features a colorful, fantasy view of the sphinx (made of snippets) at dusk, the magical moment when the world of day and night weave their edges together. Fabrics from the Cherrywood Hand-dyed Company lend the right color graduation to create the feeling of light. Photographs courtesy Fairfield.

Tranquility, 24″ x 24″, 1999, by Veronica "Ronnie" Martin. The painting "July Sunlight," by Douglas S. Grey, inspired Veronica to create this project in a Snippet class Cindy taught at the New Zealand Symposium. Veronica enjoys the Snippet technique because it has given her a way to paint with her own hand-dyed fabrics. Photographs by Jeff Mein Smith, New Zealand.

Floral Fantasy, *41″ x 31″, 1997, by Stephanie Herron Faulkner. What an exquisite piece of artwork with a lovely, aristocratic feeling! This is a perfect chance to use up fabric scraps because each flower doesn't require a large amount. Stephanie mixed and matched a wide range of color values and tones for this project. Even though she is a talented quilter, Stephanie decided to frame this project.*

Ikebana, *19″ x 21″, 1997, by Terry Matsuda Ninomura. The asymmetrical arrangement of the flowers and the shape of the vase in this flower bouquet emphasize the Asian flair.*

Yellow Glory, *24″ x 26″, 1997, Cori Rosman. This beautiful basket simply couldn't be more cheerful!*

A Passion for Perennials, *24″ x 28″, 1997, by Deanna Eicholz. What a remarkable arrangement! Deanna chose to frame this project, using a moss green mat, which perfectly complements the featured colors of green and cranberry.*

The Garden Spot, 20″ x 30″, 2000, Carol Ingram. Directions for this partial Snippet project are in Sulky Secrets to Successful Quilting (Sulky of America®), by Joyce Drexler. Carol designed and created this quilted project, which features Snippet Sensations, Crayon Art, and Sulky threads. She first used crayons to stain the fabric, creating a beautiful textile painting, and then added the snippets, machine embroidery, and free-motion quilting. The dragonfly and butterfly embellishments were created using the thread painting technique and Sulky Solvy melt-away stabilizer. Photos courtesy Sulky of America.

Lavender Jacket, 1998, by Carol Ingram. Carol is a well-known and respected garment maker. You will find several of her projects in books by Joyce Drexler of Sulky of America. She made this jacket to share with you in this book; she slightly altered the Millennium jacket pattern by Dos de Tejas to make it.

Just Three Peas and a Salad—She Whined, *24″ x 16″, 2000, by Stevii Thompson Graves. A 1999 painting by Marla Murphy, entitled "3 Damn Peas and a Salad," was Stevii's inspiration for this project. Before starting the Snippet process, she seamed the tablecloth fabric to the blue wall fabric. Notice the detail in the miniature snippet mountain scene on the wall. As the president of both the California Heritage Quilt project and Quilt San Diego—Visions, Stevii has dedicated part of her life to preserving the fine art of quilting.*

Blondie, 42″ x 42″, 2000, by Shannon Grant. During WWII, artist Don Allen painted this lady on the nose of a P-51 Mustang. Shannon first saw the airplane in a book called Nose Art, by Jeffrey L. Ethell and Clarence Simonsen (Motorbooks International). She was fascinated with this form of American military art and made this Nose Art Quilt for a group of American heroes, the CAF (Confederate Air Force) in San Diego, CA. The quilt will hang in the flying museum at the Gillespie Air Field in El Cajon, CA, for one year, beginning in 2000. The project combines several different fabrics: satin for the dress, raw silk for the wing, and cotton for the rest. To give the picture a smooth effect, she opted to use invisible thread with a sparse amount of quilting lines.

A Touch of Van Gogh, 35″ x 28″, 1997, by Cindy Walter. I wanted to create a rendition of Van Gogh's Starry Night. To capture the essence of the painting, the first thing I did was select the correct colors of fabrics, then cut the snippets in long, sweeping pieces to simulate his long brushstrokes. Rows of long, sweeping machine-quilting lines add the final touch.

Flight, 33″ x 38″, 1997, by Marilyn S. Doheny. Marilyn, an author, lecturer, and quilting instructor, grew up enchanted by nature; she would often lie on the grass, watching the clouds, birds, flowers, trees, and butterflies. In her youth, she had poor vision, so her visual memories are slightly distorted. She made this quilt the way things looked to her as a child, larger than life with images blending together. Note the use of only solid fabrics.

Davis County Covered Bridge, *26″ x 36″, 1998, by Barbara W. Barber. The snow covers all... and the cart passes through the covered bridge into eternity. Barbara, the author of* Broderie Perse *(AQS), sometimes calls this piece "Passages," because it represents the transitions in life. It was made in memory of her friend, Marilyn Davis, who loved covered bridges. Barbara used WonderUnder fusible web, and her final step was to set the project with a damp press.*

Fairy Dust, *45″ x 36″, 1998, by Deborah Sylvester. A cross-stitch pattern by Mirabilia Designs inspired Deborah to design the fairy on this quilt. Deborah made the quilt for the Camellia Quilters' Quilt Show and Challenge in Slidell, LA. It won the Viewers' Choice Award and second place in the judged show. The quilt was also featured at the Braddigins Arts and Craft Gallery, Hillsborough, NC.*

Grassicket, 41″ x 34″, 1997, by Brielyn R. Doheny. What a fun, whimsical project! At the age of 15, Brielyn was trying to create a grasshopper, but as the project progressed, people kept telling her it looked like a cricket, so she named this quilt Grassicket. Following her mother's suggestion, Brielyn added a leaf image under the creature and extended the design over the border for an artistic balance.

Kevin's Oriole, 13″ x 23″, 1997, by Cindy Wilkinson. Cindy did a fantastic job of camouflaging this realistic bird by using a rich mustard foundation. She created the branches from bamboo-printed fabric, but you could use strips of brown fabric instead.

Attic Window Garden, 48″ x 60″, 1999, by Cindy Walter. I used a 40″ x 24″ piece of hand-dyed "sky" fabric for the foundation. The flower garden was created with sweeping ferns and a variety of random flowers similar to the ones in the step-by-step flower bouquet project (page 21). Using rotary equipment, and after permanently fusing the snippets in place, I divided the foundation into 12 sections. The quilt was displayed at the Quilts in Bloom art quilt show held in the gallery of Mainau Castle, in Konstance, Germany, and featured in Attic Windows: Quilts With a View *by Diana Leone and me (Krause Publications).*

62

Earth's Gifts, *32˝ x 36˝, 1998, by Cindy Walter. This flower bouquet quilt is similar to the step-by-step flower bouquet project on page 21 (except it's larger). Add flowers of your choice, mixing and matching the fabric colors and textures. A special thanks to Northcott/Monarch Fabrics for supplying me with these beautiful fabrics called Earth Series, designed by Diana Leone.*

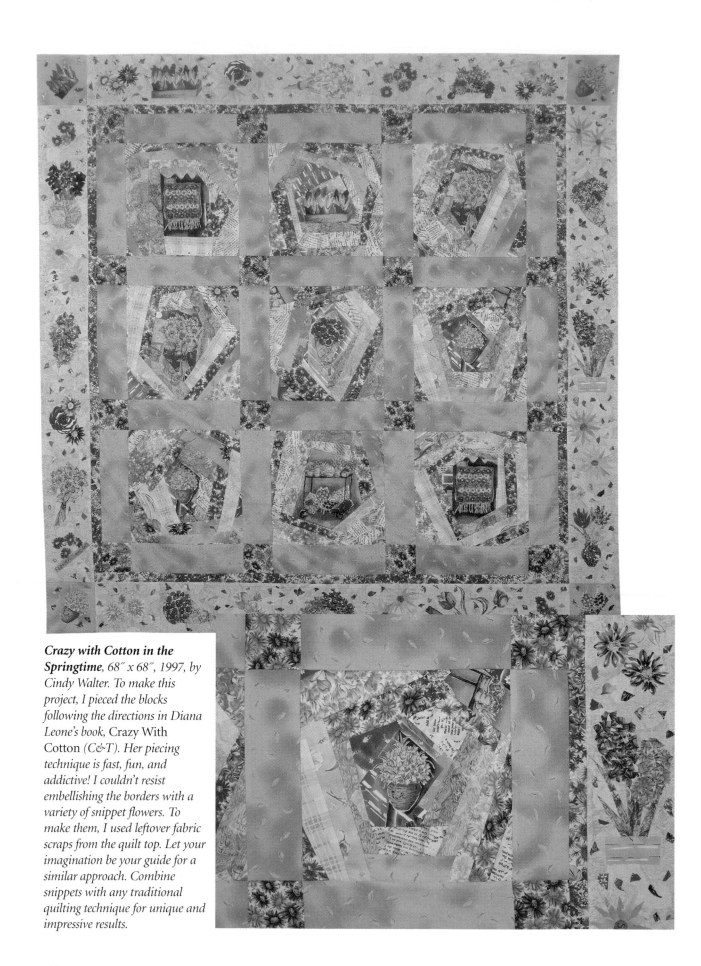

Crazy with Cotton in the Springtime, *68″ x 68″, 1997, by Cindy Walter. To make this project, I pieced the blocks following the directions in Diana Leone's book,* Crazy With Cotton *(C&T). Her piecing technique is fast, fun, and addictive! I couldn't resist embellishing the borders with a variety of snippet flowers. To make them, I used leftover fabric scraps from the quilt top. Let your imagination be your guide for a similar approach. Combine snippets with any traditional quilting technique for unique and impressive results.*

Basket of Joy on Beige, 35″ x 35″, 1996, by Cindy Walter. I made this flower bouquet quilt similar to the step-by-step project (on page 21), except this one has a cream-colored foundation. To make a similar quilt, enlarge the foundation fabric in the step-by-step project to 24″ x 24″ and make a woven basket instead of a vase. To create the basket, first pre-fuse brown fabric with fusible web. Leaving the fusible web liner paper on, and using rotary equipment, cut 18 strips 9″ long by 1/2″ wide. Cut nine of the strips in half so you have an additional 18 strips 4-1/2″ long by 1/2″ wide. Remove the fusible web paper. Stack nine long pieces horizontally on the foundation, then weave in 17 of the shorter vertical strips (as in making a lattice pie crust). A special thanks to Hoffman of California for the beautiful fabrics.

PART V Step-by-step Projects

I've included the supply lists and instructions for the following projects. For all of the projects, you will need scissors and ironing equipment. Some of them also include the measurements for borders, backing, and binding fabrics. Refer to Part III for a refresher on adding borders, sandwiching the quilt, machine quilting, and binding. Don't forget to remove the fusible web's paper liner before cutting the snippets! And, finally, remember that this is your project, and you can finish it in any desired manner. (Note: Unless otherwise stated, the projects call for 12″ wide Steam-A-Seam2.)

Seattle by Night, *30″ x 26″, 1998, by Cindy Walter. The city of Seattle is mystical at night, with colors shimmering and lights dancing on the water. Customize the buildings (such as the Twin Trade Towers in New York) to become any city. The diversity of color makes this project eye-catching; the jewel tones and uniquely shaded hand-dyes are especially exciting. Go through your fabric scrap box; this is the perfect time to use up 1″ x 2″ leftover pieces of your favorite fabrics.*

Project 1

Seattle by Night

1. Cut and iron the midnight blue foundation fabric and pre-fuse the palette fabrics. In this project, the foundation will be left partially exposed as the sky and deep blue water areas.

2. Starting with the uppermost buildings, cut rectangles (skyscrapers) of various colors and sizes.

3. Working downward, cut rectangles and squares for the middle buildings, layering these along the base and sides of the top skyscraper layer.

4. Finish with a layer of smaller, wider buildings along the waterfront.

5. This is the time to add any special "signature" building to create *your* city. To duplicate the project shown here, add the Space Needle, the signature of Seattle, by cutting three rust-colored legs and several orange and teal ovals for the top.

6. For the reflection on the water, cut thin, dark brown snippets and place them (horizontally) where the water meets the shore. Cut additional thin snippets of each of the building colors and place them horizontally in the water below the corresponding building.

7. Check to make sure all of the snippets are glue side down before fusing them permanently in place.

8. Add the borders, machine quilt, and bind.

You Will Need

Foundation Fabric	
Midnight blue	18″ x 22″
Palette Fabrics	
20 electrifying colors and	
1 brown	4″ x 4″ (each)
Steam-A-Seam2	2 yds.
Inner Border	
Orange	
Cut 2 strips:	1-1/2″ x 22″
Cut 2 strips:	1-1/2″ x 20″
Outer Border	
Blue print	
Cut 2 strips:	3-1/2″ x 24″
Cut 2 strips:	3-1/2″ x 26″
Backing Fabric	32″ x 28″
Binding Fabric	1/4 yd.
Cotton Batting	32″ x 28″

Heceta Head Celebration, 30″ x 20″, 1997, by Joyce Becker. Joyce created this Snippet landscape for her father's 80th birthday. For the back of the quilt (not shown), she transferred photographs to fabric and then appliquéd them, making a collage that features family members and special moments. What a remarkable gift!

Project 2

Heceta Head Celebration

1. Cut and iron the white foundation fabric and pre-fuse the palette fabrics. In this project, the foundation fabric will be completely covered with snippets.

2. Starting with the sky, cut random-shaped snippets from each of the cherry, red, orange, peach, and yellow fabrics and place them in the sky area; work with the darkest cherry at the top, down to yellow at the horizon. Do not use the "red roof" fabric in the sky.

3. For the water, cut long, narrow snippets from each of the blue fabrics and scatter them throughout the water area, parallel to the horizon. Show the reflection of the sky with tiny snippets of yellow and cherry fabric in the water area. Do not fill in the land areas with the blue snippets.

4. For the greenery over the ground area, cut and distribute random-shaped snippets of each of the greens.

5. For the rock area, cut and distribute random-shaped snippets of the black and brown fabrics. Reserve half of the blackest fabric to use in the lighthouse.

6. For the lighthouse, cut a large angled rectangle for the main building from the light gray fabric. You can cut this freehand or draw the building on the fusible web's paper liner. For the attached building, cut a 2″ x 3″ rectangle from the same gray and a 2″ x 5″ piece from the medium gray. Cut a slanted piece from the red roof fabric. Tuck this little building behind the lighthouse. Cut four arches from the darkest black fabric for the windows. For the spotlight, fill an area approximately 1″ x 3″ above the lighthouse with bright yellow snippets. Cut a dome for the top from the red roof fabric.

7. Use the tan fabric to create a rock in the bottom right corner.

8. Optional: Embellish the rock by fussy cutting a crane, or any other bird, positioning it on the rock.

9. Check to make sure all of the snippets are glue side down before fusing them permanently in place.

10. Following the photograph, embellish the top of the lighthouse with black cording or ribbon, attaching the embellishment with fabric glue.

11. Machine quilt and bind.

You Will Need

Foundation Fabric
  White   30″ x 20″
Palette Fabrics
  6 shades of cherry, light to
    dark   6″ x 4″ (each)
  3 shades of yellow
                      6″ x 4″ (each)
  Other sky fabrics (red, peach,
    and orange)   6″ x 6″ (each)
  6 shades of blue, light to dark
                      6″ x 6″ (each)
  4 shades of olive green
                      6″ x 6″ (each)
  3 shades of black to dark gray
                      6″ x 6″ (each)
  2 shades of dark brown
                      6″ x 6″ (each)
  Light gray   12″ x 6″
  Medium gray   6″ x 6″
  Red roof   6″ x 8″
  Tan   6″ x 4″
  Fabric with a crane or other
    bird printed on it (optional)
Black cording, 1/16″ wide, or
  ribbon   1-1/2 yds.
Steam-A-Seam2,   4 yds.
Backing Fabric   32″ x 22″
Binding Fabric   1/4 yd.
Cotton Batting   32″ x 22″
Fabric glue

Colonel Willie's Cove, 20″ x 34″, 1998, by Jennifer Priestley. *The use of fabrics from Fabrics To Dye For is the key to the drama and character of this project. Because the foundation is partially exposed, be sure to use a striking piece of fabric for that part of the project.*

You Will Need

Foundation Fabric
  Orange and pink hand-dye
  20″ x 34″

Palette Fabrics
  Bright pink   10″ x 7″
  Mauve   10″ x 7″
  Brown   12″ x 4″

Water:
  6 blues   6″ x 6″ (each)
  2 greens   6″ x 6″ (each)
  2 grays   6″ x 6″ (each)

Highlight colors (bronze, yellow,
  orange and white) 4″ x 4″ (each)
Steam-A-Seam2   2 yds.
Backing Fabric   22″ x 36″
Binding Fabric   1/4 yd.
Cotton Batting   22″ x 36″

Project 3
Colonel Willie's Cove

1. Cut and iron the sunset orange-pink foundation fabric and pre-fuse the palette fabrics. In this project, the foundation fabric will be left exposed as the sky.

2. Build the water area first by cutting long, arched snippets from the water-colored fabrics. Allow the snippet arches to reach into the sky to simulate waves. Continue cutting snippets until the water area is completely filled in.

3. Cut a long sailboat shape and a pole from the brown fabric. Cut a sail shape from each pink and place on either side of the mast. (Jennifer cleverly made the sail on the left billow in the wind by stuffing batting in the center of the sail and then fusing it down around the edges.)

4. Add a few additional water snippets to cover the bottom edge of the boat.

5. Check to make sure all of the snippets are glue side down before fusing them permanently in place.

6. Machine quilt and bind.

Field of Passion, 30″ x 50″, 1997, by Marilyn S. Doheny. This is Marilyn's first in a series of breezy, stylized floral images using Kona Bay's solid fabrics. She wanted the flowers to float and dance. The snappy yellow fabric, with the blue wind dancing through the flowers, creates a sense of believable and identifiable fun and freedom.

Project 4
Field of Passion

1. Cut and iron the foundation and pre-fuse the palette fabrics. Note: The flowers are created individually using the same general process for the stems, buds, and foliage. Their placement on the foundation is random and spontaneous. Follow the photograph for suggested placement. In this project, the vivid yellow foundation is left partially exposed as part of the design.

2. Cut arched flower stems and place them on the foundation.

3. Create the flowers by cutting softly curved arches of assorted colors.

4. Cut large arches of greens and teals for the lower foliage. For an artistic variance, allow petals from the last flower to drop on the foliage.

5. Check to make sure all of the snippets are glue side down before fusing them permanently in place.

6. Add the borders, machine quilt, and bind.

You Will Need

Foundation Fabric
  Bright yellow   22″ x 42″
Palette Fabrics
  Several assorted flower colors
                                        9″ x 18″
  Assorted greenery (chartreuse,
    dark green, medium green, and
    teal)   1/8 yd. (each)
Steam-A-Seam2   3 yds.
First Inner Border
  Dark green
        Cut 2 strips: 1-1/2″ x 22″
        Cut 2 strips: 1-1/2″ x 44″
Second Inner Border
  Medium green
        Cut 2 strips: 1″ x 24″
        Cut 2 strips: 1″ x 45-1/2″
Outer Border
  Dark green
        Cut 2 strips: 3″ x 25″
        Cut 2 strips: 3″ x 50″
Backing Fabric   32″ x 52″
Binding Fabric   1/2 yd.
Cotton Batting   32″ x 52″

Montana, *26″ x 30″, 1997, by Cindy Walter. When I got off the airplane to teach for the Stumptown Quilters' Society in Whitefish, MT, the beauty of the area took my breath away. When leaving the area, I decided to make a quilt in memory of the friends I had made in that paradise. For the correct perspective when creating a Snippet project, start with the object that is the farthest away and end with the closest. As with most landscape projects, I started with the sky at the top and simply worked downward to the grass at the bottom of the picture. Note the beautiful sky fabric made by Skydyes.*

Project 5

Montana

1. Cut and iron the white foundation fabric and pre-fuse the palette fabrics. In this project, the foundation fabric will be completely covered with panels of fabric; you will then add snippets on top of each panel.

2. Lay the pre-fused sky blue fabric on the top portion of the foundation. To use less fusible web, do not put any on the sky fabric, simply seam it to the top edge of the foundation with your sewing machine.

3. Starting in the center with the top mountain, cut 1″ x 2″ random snippets from the light blue-gray fabric and place them in a pyramid shape. Working downward, use darker shades of blue to cut mountain-shaped panels. Cover each of these areas with additional highlights of blue snippets.

4. Cut sweeping panels for the fields from the tan fabrics. Cover each of these areas with highlights of additional tan snippets.

5. Cut sweeping panels for the remaining fields from the variegated green fabric. Cover each of these areas with additional highlights of green snippets.

6. Cut tiny snippets of gold and purple to sprinkle wildflowers on selected fields.

7. Check to make sure all the snippets are glue side down before fusing them permanently in place.

8. Add the borders, machine quilt, and bind.

You Will Need

Foundation Fabric
White	18″ x 22″

Palette Fabrics
Sky blue	8″ x 18″
Navy blue	6″ x 12″
Violet blue	6″ x 12″
Dusty blue	6″ x 12″
Medium blue	6″ x 6″
Warm tan	6″ x 12″
Cool tan	6″ x 12″

4 greens, from light to dark
          12″ x 6″ (each)

Lime green, purple, orange
          4″ x 4″ (each)

Steam-A-Seam2	3 yds.

Inner Border
Brown	
Cut 2 strips:	1-1/2″ x 22″
Cut 2 strips:	1-1/2″ x 20″

Outer Border
Blue print	
Cut 2 strips:	3-1/2″ x 24″
Cut 2 strips:	3-1/2″ x 26″

Backing Fabric	28″ x 32″
Binding Fabric	1/4 yd.
Cotton Batting	28″ x 32″

The Old Collins Place, *32″ x 24″, 1996, by Barbara W. Barber. I was honored when I learned of Barbara's interest in the Snippet technique. WonderUnder is her fusible webbing of choice. Different shades of white and gray create the perfect illusion of snow. Photo by Hiram W. Barber.*

Project 6

The Old Collins Place

1. Cut and iron the white foundation and pre-fuse the palette fabrics. In this project, the foundation will be completely covered with snippets.

2. For the sky area, use the medium gray fabrics. Cut and place random snippets until it is completely filled in.

3. Create fir trees with small, sweeping snippets of the dark gray fabric.

4. Create the barn with random-shaped snippets from the two brown fabrics. Notice that the light is coming from the left, so use the lighter brown on surfaces facing the left and the darker brown on surfaces facing the right. Use a variety of off-white and tan fabrics for the roof.

5. Create the snow-covered ground by cutting snippets from the lightest off-white fabrics. Place them on the left-hand side of the picture, working into tan fabrics (in the furrows of the snow drifts) on the right.

6. Build a large tree trunk on the right-hand side of the picture, using vertical snippets from the black fabrics. Place a few off-white snow snippets in the crooks of the branches; also cover the bottom of the tree with snow.

7. Make two fence rails from long snippets of the black and dark gray fabrics. Place the rails at an angle across the bottom third of the picture (they do not have to be parallel). Add small snippets of light gray and off-white fabrics to create mounds of snow across the tops of the rails. Make two fence posts from long, thin snippets of the medium gray fabrics on the left, going into black fabric on the right. Place a mound of snow on top of each post with snippets of light gray and off-white fabrics.

8. Check to make sure all of the snippets are glue side down before fusing them permanently in place.

9. Add the borders, machine quilt, and bind.

You Will Need

Foundation Fabric
White   18″ x 26″
Palette Fabrics
   10 shades of gray, light to
      dark   6″ x 6″ (each)
    6 shades of black   6″ x 6″ (each)
    4 light tans   6″ x 6″ (each)
    6 off-whites   6″ x 6″ (each)
    2 browns   6″ x 6″ (each)
Steam-A-Seam2   3 yds.
or
WonderUnder, 18″ wide   2 yds.
Inner Border
   Dark gray
          Cut 2 strips: 1″ x 26″
          Cut 2 strips: 1″ x 19″
Middle Border
   Light gray
        Cut 2 strips: 1-1/2″ x 27″
        Cut 2 strips: 1-1/2″ x 21″
Outer Border
   Brown print
        Cut 2 strips: 2″ x 29″
        Cut 2 strips: 2″ x 24″
Backing Fabric   34″ x 26″
Binding Fabric   1/4 yd.
Cotton Batting   34″ x 26″

Sunny Summer Afternoon, *34″ x 40″, 1996, by Jo Anne Robertson. Jo Anne's inspiration for this sunny project came from a greeting card. Using green leaf-printed fabric for the foundation was a great idea because it shows through in many areas of the project, eliminating the need for numerous snippets. This quilt won a second place Viewers Choice award in the small, contemporary quilt category in 1998 at the Block Party Quilters Show in Bellevue, WA.*

Project 7

Sunny Summer Afternoon

1. Cut and iron the green foundation fabric and pre-fuse the palette fabrics. In this project, the green leaf print fabric foundation fabric will occasionally show through as a partially exposed foundation.

2. Starting with the upper half, cut random-shaped snippets from each of the "background" fabrics and place them in strips across the upper area in this order: medium green, tan, medium green, and yellow. Allow the foundation fabric to show through as much as desired. Reserve small amounts of each green fabric and a large portion of the tan fabric to use later for the ground area.

3. For the tree, cut a large trunk and long, sweeping branches from the brown fabric. Highlight the tree with smaller snippets of the light and dark browns.

4. Create the fence. For the pickets, cut 1/2″ wide snippets, approximately 4″ tall, from the various tan and off-white fabrics. Notice that the pickets directly beneath the tree are darker (in the shade of the tree), and off to either side they get lighter. Shade the pickets with thin snippets of complementary fabrics. Cut thin strips of the lightest tans to create the rail that runs horizontally across the pickets.

5. Fill in the grass area and the leaves of the tree using the remaining green fabrics. For the grass, cut thin snippets of various greens and place them vertically throughout the entire bottom portion of the project, overlapping the bottoms of the fence pickets. Use mint green fabric as a highlight on the right-hand side of the grass. Cut random snippets of the remaining greens to create the leaves on the tree.

6. For the field flowers, cut tiny snippets of the various white and peach fabrics; sprinkle these densely throughout the grass area. Add highlights of yellow and lavender snippets.

7. Check to make sure all of the snippets are glue side down before fusing them permanently in place.

8. Add the borders, machine quilt, and bind.

You Will Need

Foundation Fabric	
Green leaf print	24″ x 30″
Palette Fabrics	
6 shades of green	6″ x 6″ (each)
2 shades of mint green	
	6″ x 6″ (each)
Medium brown	12″ x 6″
Dark and light brown	
	6″ x 6″ (each)
Medium tan	12″ x 6″
Light and dark tan	6″ x 6″ (each)
2 off-whites	6″ x 6″ (each)
4 whites	6″ x 6″ (each)
2 shades of salmon	6″ x 6″ (each)
2 yellows	6″ x 6″ (each)
Lavender	6″ x 6″
Steam-A-Seam2	3 yds.
Inner Border	
Dark brown	
	Cut 2 strips: 1″ x 30″
	Cut 2 strips: 1″ x 25″
Outer Border	
Green	
	Cut 2 strips: 4″ x 31″
	Cut 2 strips: 4″ x 32″
Backing Fabric	36″ x 42″
Binding Fabric	1/4 yd.
Cotton Batting	36″ x 42″

Sidewalk Café, *23˝ x 18˝, 1998, by Cindy Walter. A Vincent Van Gogh painting was the inspiration for this project, in which fabric selection is the key to success. The unique fabrics used here were provided by Fabrics To Dye For (see Sources and Suppliers). To create the illusion of movement, I not only free-motion quilted swirls in the sky, but I also added additional "cobblestone" snippets on the borders.*

Project 8

Sidewalk Café

1. Cut and iron the white foundation and pre-fuse the palette and panel fabrics. In this project, the foundation fabric will be completely covered with panels and then snippets of fabric.

2. Set the blue sky fabric on the top portion of the foundation.

3. Place the mint green fabric across the bottom portion of the foundation (overlapping the bottom edge of the blue fabric).

4. Using the dark blue fabric, cut various squares and rectangles to create the buildings on the right.

5. To start the building on the left, place a 3-1/2″ x 3-1/2″ piece of baby blue fabric in the top left corner.

6. For the main building on the left, cut a large, angled piece of bright yellow fabric as the awning and a yellow square for the building, tucking the building under the awning. Place a strip of lime green shading along the left side of the building. Create an archway from the dark blue fabric. Cut a wedge for the rug and a rectangle for the door from the orange fabric. Make several tables, cutting an oval of blue fabric for the tabletop and three thin strips of brown fabric for the legs.

7. To finish the building on the right, cut a variety of yellow and green squares or rectangles of all sizes to create windows and doors.

8. To create the tree, which is hanging over the right-hand side of the building, cut small, thin snippets of lime and medium green fabric.

9. Cut small "clothespin" shapes for the people, filling in their details with a fine-tipped fabric pen.

10. Check to make sure all of the snippets are glue side down before fusing them permanently in place.

11. Add the borders.

12. Cut small, arched snippets of all colors and add to the street area for cobblestones. Allow the cobblestones to filter out into the borders.

13. Once again, fuse all new snippets permanently in place.

14. Machine quilt and bind.

You Will Need

Foundation Fabric
White	16″ x 11″

Palette Fabrics
Sky blue	11-1/2″ x 8″
Mint green	11-1/2″ x 9″
Dark blue	12″ x 6″
Bright yellow	8″ x 6″
Lime green	8″ x 6″
Orange	8″ x 6″
Baby blue	6″ x 6″
Brown	6″ x 6″
Rust	6″ x 6″
Steam-A-Seam2	2 yds.

Inner Border
Orange
Cut 2 strips: 1-1/2″ x 16″
Cut 2 strips: 1-1/2″ x 13″

Outer Border
Blue
Cut 4 strips: 3″ x 18″

Backing Fabric	25″ x 20″
Binding Fabric	1/4 yd.
Cotton Batting	25″ x 20″

Fine-tipped permanent fabric pen

Black Tulips, *25″ x 29″, 1997, by Anne Anderson. Anne, who painted the silk fabrics for this framed project, is a fiber artist by trade. The foundation fabric is cotton, but the rest of the design is made with her hand-painted silk. Feel free to use cotton or silk, or any combination of fabrics, in your project.*

Project 9

Black Tulips

1. Prepare the foundation and pre-fuse the palette fabrics. In this project, the black marbled foundation fabric will be partially exposed behind the lime green ground cover.

2. Start by filling in the foundation with random-shaped snippets of lime green. Sprinkle additional snippets of brown and darker green for depth.

3. Cut long, sweeping stems and chunky leaves from the various greens. Position them on top of the lime green.

4. For the tulips, cut nine oval pieces of various sizes from the very dark cherry. Put these in position at the top of the stems. Cut and layer on strips of the medium dark, medium, and then light cherry to add dimension to the tulips.

5. Check to make sure all of the snippets are glue side down before fusing them permanently in place.

You Will Need

Foundation Fabric
Black marbled   17″ x 21″
Palette Fabrics
  3 shades of mint green, from
    light to dark   6″ x 12″ (each)
  3 shades of lime green, from light
    to dark   12″ x 12″ (each)
  3 shades of cherry, from light to
    medium dark   4″ x 4″ (each)
  Very dark cherry   6″ x 6″
  Brown   4″ x 4″
Steam-A-Seam2   1-1/2 yds.

Rite of Spring, 30″ x 24″, 1997, by Pam Vonhof. Pam loves to hand dye fabric as a hobby. She used her own hand-dyed fabrics and fabrics made by Judy Robinson to create this spectacular project. The drama of the composition is very inspiring.

Project 10

Rite of Spring

1. Cut and iron the foundation and pre-fuse the palette fabrics. In this project, the foundation will be exposed.

2. Cut long, sweeping branches from the brown fabric, draping them from the sky.

3. Scatter snippet leaves from each of the green fabrics along the branches.

4. Create fuchsias by cutting snippets from the purple, pink, and blue fabrics, overlapping them in a circular fashion.

5. Check to make sure all of the snippets are glue side down before fusing them permanently in place.

6. Add the borders, machine quilt, and bind.

You Will Need

Foundation Fabric
  Light green hand-dyed   16″ x 22″
Palette Fabrics
  Brown   12″ x 6″
  4 shades of green   4″ x 4″ (each)
  6 shades purple and pink
                       4″ x 4″ (each)
  Blue   4″ x 4″
Steam-A-Seam2   1 yd.
Inner Border
  Blue
            Cut 2 strips: 1-1/2″ x 22″
            Cut 2 strips: 1-1/2″ x 18″
Outer Border
  Blue print
            Cut 4 strips: 3-1/2″ x 24″
Backing Fabric   32″ x 26″
Binding Fabric   1/4 yd.
Cotton Batting   32″ x 26″

A Snippet of Sunflowers, *30″ x 33″, 1997, by Karen Wang. What a beautiful color combination of lime green, golden yellow, and periwinkle! Karen is a wonderful seamstress who enjoys teaching children how to sew.*

Project 11

A Snippet of Sunflowers

1. Cut and iron the foundation and pre-fuse the palette fabrics. In this project, the beige foundation will be exposed behind the bouquet.

2. Make the vase from the periwinkle fabric.

3. Cut long, sweeping snippets from the green fabrics for the leaves. Set them in place, tucking the ends under the top of the vase. Also cut large leaf shapes from each of the green fabrics. Fill in the background with green foliage.

4. Start with the sunflower in the center. To make sunflowers, cut 10 spears 1-1/2˝ long from each golden yellow fabric and place them in a large circle, leaving the center empty. Cut random-shaped snippets from two of the brown fabrics, creating a dark mound in the center of each flower. Repeat the process five times for the other sunflowers, varying the lightness and darkness of the yellows and browns.

5. Check to make sure all of the snippets are glue side down before fusing them permanently in place.

6. Add the borders, machine quilt, and bind.

You Will Need

Foundation Fabric
Beige   21˝ x 24˝
Palette Fabrics
Periwinkle (for vase)   9˝ x 9˝
5 greens (from light lime to dark)
                         6˝ x 6˝ (each)
4 golden yellows   6˝ x 6˝ (each)
3 browns   4˝ x 4˝ (each)
Steam-A-Seam2   2 yds.
Inner Border
Lime green
         Cut 2 strips: 1-1/2˝ x 24˝
         Cut 2 strips: 1-1/2˝ x 23˝
Outer Border
Periwinkle
            Cut 2 strips: 4˝ x 26˝
            Cut 2 strips: 4˝ x 30˝
Backing Fabric   32˝ x 35˝
Binding Fabric   1/4 yd.
Cotton Batting   32˝ x 35˝

Autumn, *32″ x 28″, 1997, by Pam Vonhof. Pam's one-of-a-kind hand-dyed fabrics make this a gorgeous project. Once the palette fabrics are selected, the project can be created very quickly. It has an exposed foundation with specifically shaped snippets on bottom that create the image. Start with an exceptionally beautiful piece of fabric for the foundation; it will dominate the mood of the picture.*

Project 12

*A*utumn

1. Cut and iron the yellow foundation and pre-fuse the palette fabrics. In this project, the foundation fabric will be left exposed as the golden sky behind the foliage.

2. Using a compass or kitchen plate, cut a 10″ diameter circle for the sun out of the orange-red fabric.

3. For the leaf stems, cut 6″ long, thin snippets of gray fabric.

4. For the foliage, cut brown leaf-shaped snippets and place them along the stems.

5. Check to make sure all of the snippets are glue side down before fusing them permanently in place.

6. Add the borders, machine quilt, and bind.

Note: This project has a series of four borders sets. The first border strip is on the top and bottom only, not on the sides.

You Will Need

Foundation Fabric	
Yellow marbled	12″ x 18″
Palette Fabrics	
Orange-red (sun)	12″ x 12″
2 warm grays	6″ x 6″ (each)
Green	6″ x 6″
Steam-A-Seam2	1 yd.
Liner Border	
Brown	
	Cut 2: 1-1/2″ x 18-1/2″
Inner Border	
Rust	
	Cut 4: 2-1/2″ x 18″
Middle Border	
Brown	
	Cut 2 strips: 2″ x 22″
	Cut 2 strips: 2″ x 21″
Outer Border	
Orange print	
	Cut 2 strips: 4″ x 25″
	Cut 2 strips: 4″ x 28″
Backing Fabric	34″ x 30″
Binding Fabric	1/4 yd.
Cotton Batting	34″ x 30″
Compass or 10″ round kitchen plate to create a circle	

Autograph Wreath, 22″ x 28″, 1996, by Rebecca "Bekki" Mae Redfearn. As Cindy's niece, part-time assistant, and constant supporter, Bekki is surround by Snippet Sensations. Almost daily, she points to something and says, "Aunt Cindy, that would make a great Snippet project." Her autograph wreath is a fantastic idea. Simply follow the plans for Rochelle's Wreath, using the colors of your choice. Cut the snippets wider and longer than normal so there is room to write on them. After fusing the snippets permanently in place, pass the wreath and a permanent fabric pen around to your friends, encouraging them to write cherished memories.

Aloha Lei, 26″ x 32″, 1998, by Cindy Walter. I call this my "cheater quilt" because it is so fast and fun to create. Simply choose floral fabrics and a highly contrasting foundation fabric. Pre-fuse the floral fabrics with fusible web, fussy-cut individual flowers, and then arrange them in a lei pattern. For this quilt, I used special fabrics purchased in Hawaii.

Rochelle's Wreath, 27″ x 22″, 1997, by Rochelle Savage. Rochelle is the owner of Rochelle's Fine Fabrics in Port Orchard, WA. As you can see, she is a talented quilter who has a great eye for color and fabrics.

Project 13

Rochelle's Wreath

1. Cut and iron the white foundation fabric and pre-fuse the palette fabrics. In this project, the foundation fabric shows behind the wreath as part of the design.

2. Cut large (1″ x 4″), sweeping snippets of the green, purple, and blue fabrics. Arrange them in a circle. Continue cutting snippets until the wreath is the desired size and shape.

3. Make poinsettias from the multi-print and red fabrics by cutting a large circle from the brighter fabrics. Then, from these circular pieces, cut thin, long, arched snippets (1/4″ x 4″) and place them in gathered circles.

4. Sprinkle tiny snippets of gold in the centers of the flowers. For sparkle, add additional snippets of gold throughout the wreath.

5. Check to make sure all of the snippets are glue side down before fusing them permanently in place.

6. Add the borders, machine quilt, and bind.

You Will Need

Foundation Fabric	
White	21″ x 16″
Palette Fabrics	
4 greens, from light to dark	
	6″ x 6″ (each)
2 purples, 2 blues, 2 multi colors, and 2 reds	6″ x 6″ (each)
Gold	6″ x 6″
Steam-A-Seam2	1-1/2 yds.
Inner Border	
Green	
	Cut 2 strips: 1″ x 21″
	Cut 2 strips: 1″ x 17″
Inner Border	
Print	
	Cut 4 strips: 3″ x 22″
Backing Fabric	29″ x 24″
Binding Fabric	1/4 yd.
Cotton Batting	29″ x 24″

89

Christmas Celebration, *27″ x 31″, 1999, by Cindy Walter. This quilt features fussy-cut gifts under a simple, yet striking, tree.*

Project 14

Christmas Celebration

You Will Need

Foundation Fabric
  White   22″ x 18″
Palette Fabrics
  4 to 6 greens   6″ x 12″ (each)
  Christmas theme print   1/8 yd.
Steam-A-Seam2   1 yd.
Inner border
  Red
            Cut 2 strips: 1-1/2″ x 22″
            Cut 2 strips: 1-1/2″ x 20″
Outer border
  Print
            Cut 2 strips: 4″ x 24″
            Cut 2 strips: 4″ x 27″
Backing Fabric   29″ x 33″
Binding Fabric   1/4 yd.
Cotton Batting   29″ x 33″

1. Cut and iron the white foundation and pre-fuse the palette fabrics. In this project, the foundation will be partially exposed behind the colorful tree.

2. Cut random-shaped spears from the green fabrics. Place one vertically at the very top of the tree. Working downward, spread out the snippets.

3. Continue to work downward, interchanging the different green fabrics until the tree is completed.

4. Cut circles for the ornaments from the Christmas fabric and fussy cut motifs from the Christmas fabrics to decorate under the tree.

5. Check to make sure all of the snippets are glue side down before fusing them permanently in place.

6. Add the borders, machine quilt, and bind.

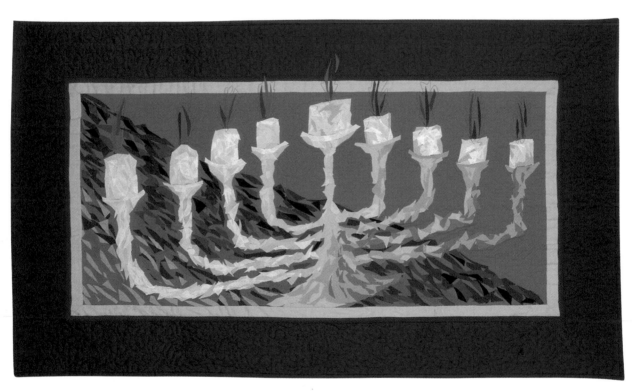

Burning Remembrance, 32″ x 48″, 1997, by Brielyn R. Doheny. Brielyn's mother made quilts for Kona Bay using their beautiful collection of solid fabrics. At the age of 15, Brielyn was taken by the fabrics and decided to use them to honor the Jewish religion. In her first attempt, she was one arm short of the menorah's nine arms. Thanks to the Snippet technique, she realized it was easy to instantly add another arm.

Project 15

Burning Remembrance

1. Cut and iron the blue foundation fabric and pre-fuse the palette fabrics. In this project, the sky blue fabric will be completely exposed across the top and partially exposed behind the sweeping background snippets of blue, black, teal, and lavender.

2. Create the pedestal and the nine "arms" of the menorah first. Notice the light source is coming from the left side of the scene. The arms on the left are made from the lightest yellow; they gradually get darker as they move across to the right side. Cut random-shaped snippets from yellow, tan, and rust fabric to build the pedestal and nine arms.

3. Place candles on top of the arms by cutting random snippets from the white, mint green, and light pink fabrics. Each flame is constructed from three long, thin snippets. The flame on the candle at the left is orange. Gradually mix the orange and red fabrics until the last flame on the right is entirely red.

4. Create the background by cutting and placing long, thin snippets of the blue, black, teal, and lavender fabrics, sweeping diagonally behind the menorah. Note: For this project, we are working in an odd order (creating the background after the image). This is because the darker background fabrics cannot be behind the wispy, light fabrics in the menorah.

5. Check to make sure all the snippets are glue side down before fusing them permanently in place.

6. Add the borders, machine quilt, and bind.

You Will Need

Foundation Fabric	
Sky blue	20″ x 36″
Palette Fabrics	
2 dark blues	12″ x 6″ (each)
Gray blue	12″ x 6″
Light blue	12″ x 6″
Dark teal, lavender, and black	6″ x 6″ (each)
3 yellows, from light to dark	12″ x 6″ (each)
Tan	12″ x 6″
Light rust	8″ x 6″
4 reds, from burgundy to orange	6″ x 6″ (each)
White, light mint green, and light pink	6″ x 6″ (each)
Steam-A-Seam2	3 yds.
Inner Border	
Yellow	
Cut 2 strips: 1-1/2″ x 36″	
Cut 2 strips: 1-1/2″ x 22″	
Middle Border	
Red	
Cut 2 strips: 1″ x 38″	
Cut 2 strips: 1″ x 23″	
Outer Border	
Royal blue	
Cut 2 strips: 5″ x 39″	
Cut 2 strips: 5″ x 32″	
Backing Fabric	34″ x 50″
Binding Fabric	1/4 yd.
Cotton Batting	34″ x 50″

Millennium Jacket, 1999, by
Marilyn Donahoe. Marilyn is a
wonderful seamstress, who is always
creating a new "wearable art"
garment. Her husband Dick helps her
design the projects. That is right, he
actually goes to the store with her and
helps pick out the fabrics, buttons,
and embellishments. (Is the cloning
process ready to test on humans yet?)
Marilyn made her jacket with a
pattern from Belinda's Designs. Vary
the fabric needed according to the
jacket pattern, and size, of your
choice. Because this project was made
for the new millennium, all of the
fabrics have tiny stars printed on
them. Vary the theme of your jacket
to correspond with any event.

Project 16

Millennium Jacket

1. In this project, you will embellish a "store-bought" jacket pattern. Read through the instructions that come with the pattern. Cut out the jacket pattern, allowing 1″ extra all of the way around. Back each piece of the pattern (except the lining and any interfacings) with the lightweight fleece.

2. Channel or stipple quilt 3/4″ apart with light blue thread on each piece. When all of the pieces are quilted, re-cut the pattern pieces according to the pattern dimensions.

3. Pre-fuse about 1/8 yard of each blue fabric and the silver lamé with Steam-A-Seam2.

4. Cut snippets in long, random shapes to create the burst in the center of the back panel and to the front panels.

5. Check to make sure all of the snippets are glue side down before fusing them permanently in place.

6. Complete the jacket by following the pattern instructions to sew the sections together.

You Will Need

Jacket pattern of your choice

Black cotton for the jacket and blue satin for the lining, yardage as needed according to the pattern

Lightweight fleece for the padding 2 yds.

3 shades of blue 1/4 yd. (each)

Silver lamé (the type you can iron with the easy knit backing)
1/4 yd.

Steam-A-Seam2   2 yds.

Light blue cotton quilting thread

Gray, or neutral, piecing thread

Caribbean Memories, *42″ x 42″, 1997, by Leone Newman. Leone made this whimsical picture to hang above the Jacuzzi in her bathroom. What a fun, playful project! It is easy to change the overall size of the project because it doesn't have borders, so vary fabric amounts according to your needs.*

Project 17

Caribbean Memories

1. Cut and iron the foundation fabric and pre-fuse the palette fabrics. In this project, the marbled, hand-dyed foundation fabric will be exposed throughout, behind the water snippets.

2. To shade the water, cut long, thin snippets of the water fabrics and place them horizontally. Place the darker blue and gray fabrics on the right and left side of the foundation, and the lighter grays, blues, yellow, and pink fabrics at an angle down the middle to simulate a ray of light.

3. Cut long, sweeping reeds from the green fabric, about 2″ thick and the length of the fabric. Do not fuse these in place, because several of the fish will be tucked behind the reeds.

4. Freely cut fish of all shapes from the 12 colors. Each fish can be one color or a mixture of several colors. Tuck several of the fish behind the reeds. Embellish the fish with additional fabric snippets or fine-tipped fabric pens.

5. Add the rocks by cutting large, sweeping panels of the dark fabrics, layering downward to the bottom.

6. Check to make sure all of the snippets are glue side down before fusing permanently in place.

7. Machine quilt and bind.

You Will Need

Foundation Fabric
  Marbled, hand-dyed   42″ x 42″
Palette Fabrics
  Medium green   36″ x 12″
  2 light greens   12″ x 12″ (each)
Water shading:
  4 blues, from light to royal
                        6″ x 6″ (each)
  3 grays, from light to dark
                        6″ x 6″ (each)
  Pink   6″ x 6″
  Yellow   6″ x 6″
Rocks:
  Dark gray   12″ x 6″
  Dark blue   12″ x 6″
  Purple   12″ x 6″
Fish:
  12 different electric colors
                       10″ x 6″ (each)
Steam-A-Seam2   6 yds.
Backing Fabric   44″ x 44″
Binding Fabric   1/4 yd.
Cotton Batting   44″ x 44″
Permanent fabric pen (optional)

Giraffe: A Newborn, *36˝ x 30˝, 1997, by David Small. David is a quilt designer, quilting teacher, and the author of the book* Quilt Foundations: Sewing on the Lines *(Small Expressions). He did a fabulous job on this project. The border is made from snippets added on top of the foundation; he did not sew additional borders onto the project!*

Project 18

Giraffe: A Newborn

1. Cut and iron the foundation fabric and pre-fuse the palette fabrics. In this project, the white foundation will be completely covered with snippets.

2. Because you are adding a 2″ border of snippets, start the project 2″ in from the edges of the foundation. Create the background behind the giraffe by completely covering the foundation fabric with large, random-shaped snippets from the four sky blues, two tree greens, two grass greens, light brown, and rusts. Fuse the background in place.

3. To create the body and legs, cut large, 4″ random-shaped snippets from the light, medium, and dark tan fabrics. Use the darkest tan for the head. Move the snippets around until the general shape of the giraffe is formed.

4. Cut uneven, circular dark tan snippets and place them on the body for the spots. Use the golden tans for the spots on the legs.

5. For the mane, cut spiky golden tan snippets and place them down the back.

6. Cut two wedges for the ears from the lighter tan fabric and a small piece of black fabric by the top ear for the horn.

7. For the eyes, cut a black oval; create the lids on the top and bottom with slits of light tan fabric.

8. Cut two slits of light tan for the nostril and mouth.

9. To create the finishing touch, the snippet border, cut large, random snippets from the gray-bronze fabric and create a 2″ thick border around the perimeter of the foundation.

10. Check to make sure all of the snippets are glue side down before fusing them permanently in place.

11. Machine quilt and bind.

You Will Need

Foundation Fabric
White	30″ x 36″

Palette Fabrics
4 light sky blues	12″ x 12″ (each)
2 tree greens	12″ x 12″ (each)
2 grass greens	12″ x 12″ (each)
Light brown	12″ x 12″
Light orange-rust print	12″ x 12″
Medium orange-rust print	
	12″ x 12″

Giraffe:
Dark and medium tans	
	24″ x 12″ (each)
Light tan	12″ x 12″
2 golden tans	6″ x 6″ (each)
Black	6″ x 6″

Border
Gray-bronze	24″ x 12″
Steam-A-Seam2	7 yds.
Backing Fabric	32″ x 38″
Binding Fabric	1/4 yd.
Cotton Batting	32″ x 38″

Panda, *24˝ x 36˝, 1997, by Ellen Taylor Suffern. This exotic panda bear looms larger than life in its bamboo forest. What an excellent use of fabric! Notice that Ellen chose a bamboo print to border her project. She felt the Snippet technique was well suited to the shagginess of the panda's fur, as well as for creating the sunlight and shadows in the forest.*

Project 19

Panda

1. Cut and iron the foundation fabric and pre-fuse the palette fabrics. In this project, the green print foundation fabric will be partially exposed behind the other green forest fabrics in the background.

2. Sprinkle random snippets from the two green fabrics over the foundation to create the forest background. Allow the foundation to show through as part of the forest.

3. For the panda's shoulder and body, cut a large piece (or several layered pieces) of dark gray. To create fur, cover the dark gray base with thin snippets of the black and brown fabrics. For the head, cut an oval shape from the tan fabric. Also cut two ears from the tan fabric. Create fur on the head with thin, off-white snippets, starting at the center of the face and radiating outward in a circle. For the eye area, cut two kidney bean shapes from black fabric. Add two black circles for the eyes. Cut black nostrils and a burgundy oval for the mouth area. Add a pink oval to the center of the mouth for the tongue and cut cream colored spikes for the teeth.

4. Cut a long strip of green to create the bamboo coming from the panda's mouth.

5. To create the hand that is holding the bamboo, add a few brown snippets over the bamboo, about 4″ down from the mouth.

6. Check to make sure all of the snippets are glue side down before fusing them permanently in place.

7. Add the borders, machine quilt, and bind.

You Will Need

Foundation Fabric
  Green print — 28″ x 16″
Palette Fabrics
  3 greens — 6″ x 6″ (each)
  Dark gray — 18″ x 12″
  2 blacks — 12″ x 8″ (each)
  2 browns — 6″ x 6″ (each)
  Tan — 14″ x 12″
  Dark tan — 6″ x 6″
  2 off-whites — 8″ x 6″ (each)
  Burgundy — 4″ x 4″
  Pink — 4″ x 4″
  Cream — 4″ x 4″
Steam-A-Seam2 — 3 yds.
Inner Border
  Tan print
    Cut 2 strips: 1-1/2″ x 28″
    Cut 2 strips: 1-1/2″ x 18-1/2″
Outer Border
  Green print
    Cut 2 strips: 3-1/4″ x 30-1/2″
    Cut 2 strips: 3-1/4″ x 24″
Backing Fabric — 38″ x 26″
Binding Fabric — 1/4 yd.
Cotton Batting — 38″ x 26″

Leone Cub*, 29″ x 29″, 1997, by Eddie Leone Jr. Eddie's creative talents are evident in this superb piece. He used tweezers to place each tiny piece of the cub's fur in place. The green printed fabric made a perfect partially exposed foundation.*

Project 20

Leone Cub

1. Cut and iron the foundation fabric and pre-fuse the palette fabrics. In this project, the green foundation print is exposed behind the other green forest fabrics in the background.

2. Create the forest background first by cutting long snippets from each of the green fabrics. Use the darker green fabrics at the top of the picture. Place most of the green snippets vertically to give the appearance of grass. Allow the green foundation to show through as much as desired. Reserve half of the darkest greens to use in the cub's shadow area.

3. For the cub, cut large chunks, or panels, from the brown fabrics and place them so they create a silhouette of the cub's body. (This is really easier than it sounds!) If you desire, draw a silhouette of the cub's body on a piece of paper to use as a guideline. Cutting large chunks, or panels, of fabric is the easiest method because when you add tiny, thin snippets on top of these chunks, it will look like you cut hundreds of snippets (when you really only precision-cut the top layer). Create the fur with thin snippets of fabric. Use dark brown and dabs of black on the left-hand side in the shaded area, dark golden tan throughout most of the body, and the lightest tan on the right-hand side where the light is reflecting. Alternate the colors of the snippets to give the fur texture. Also, use the snippet colors to create two front legs and a back leg. Continue in the same manner on the cub's face. Make most of the face dark tan; shade parts of the left side with dark brown and parts of the right side with light tan.

4. From the black fabric, cut two almond-shaped eyes, a slit for the nose and mouth, and two arches for the inner ears. Using the lightest tan fabric, cut long, thin snippets to create the eyebrows and whiskers and also to highlight in and around the eyes.

5. Check to make sure all the snippets are glue side down before fusing them permanently in place.

6. Add the borders, machine quilt, and bind.

You Will Need

Foundation Fabric
  Forest green print   22″ x 22″
Palette Fabrics
  6 greens, from very dark to
    medium   6″ x 6″ (each)
  Dark brown   12″ x 6″
  Brown   12″ x 6″
  Dark golden tan   12″ x 6″
  Black   6″ x 6″
  4 tans, from very light to medium
        6″ x 6″ (each)
Steam-A-Seam2   2 yds.
Outer Border (not shown)
  Green print
        Cut 2 strips: 4″ x 22″
        Cut 2 strips: 4″ x 29″
Backing Fabric   31″ x 31″
Binding Fabric   1/4 yd.
Cotton Batting   31″ x 31″

Little Dutch Boy, *50″ x 50″, 1997, by Kristine Calney and Susan Kinyon. The Heritage Trail Keeshond Club of Massachusetts hosted a national show for the Keeshond Club of America in 1997. This remarkable quilt was made for an auction on behalf of the club. A traditionally pieced border surrounds the snippet Keeshond dog. You can combine any piecing methods with your Snippet creation. The instructions are for the center medallion only; add borders as desired.*

Project 21

Little Dutch Boy

You Will Need
(for the center square)

Foundation Fabric	
White	20″ x 20″
Palette Fabrics	
2 black prints	6″ x 6″ (each)
5 grays, from dark to very light	6″ x 6″ (each)
Dark pink	4″ x 4″
Burgundy	4″ x 4″
Steam-A-Seam2	1 yd.

1. Cut and iron the foundation fabric and pre-fuse the palette fabrics. In this project, the whole white foundation is exposed behind the dog, then the entire project is pieced in the center of a larger quilt.

2. Cut long, thin snippets from the lighter gray fabrics. Alternating the grays, place the snippets in a large circle, working inward. Place a layer of the darkest grays and the black fabrics in a circle, to give the dog's head definition. Continue to alternate the gray and black fabrics, filling in the animal's entire face.

3. For the ears, place two gray wedges on the top of the head; add small pink ovals to the centers.

4. Cut a black nose.

5. Cut oval burgundy eyes with tiny black circles in the centers.

6. Cut a burgundy oval for the mouth and add another pink oval on top for the tongue.

7. Check to make sure all of the snippets are glue side down before fusing them permanently in place.

8. Add this block into the center of any type of quilt.

Waiting for the Dragonfly, *40″ x 48″, 1997, by Marilyn Berg. Marilyn's fabric selection makes this an especially beautiful quilt. Create the bird of your choice by changing the fabric colors and body shape.*

Great Blue Heron, *24″ x 27″, 1999, by Laverne Mathews. Here is a variation of the heron project above. Laverne started it in a Snippet class with Cindy in Beaumont, TX. The following year, Laverne brought the project back to Cindy's class. Laverne wasn't happy with the quilt, feeling it lacked spark, so Cindy used it to demonstrate to the class how to add movement with quilting lines. As a result, the heron came to life!*

Project 22

Waiting for the Dragonfly

1. Cut and iron the foundation fabric and pre-fuse the palette and panel fabrics. In this project, large panels of fabric cover the foundation.

2. Create the background first by laying the top sky panel across the top of the foundation. Then, lay the center sky panel in the center of the project.

3. Cut the wine-colored hill panels in sweeping hill shapes and place them so they create mountains, hiding the bottom edge of the center sky panel.

4. Lay the water panel so it covers the bottom edge of the mountain panels.

5. Create the heron by cutting large chunks from the gray fabrics, placing them to create the body shape. Cut large, soft wedges from the pink fabrics to create the wings and the face area. Create the feathered crown by cutting and placing alternating snippets of the lightest and then darkest gray fabrics. Cut a tiny circle from the darkest gray fabric for the eye. Cut a pointed beak from the light brown fabric. Cut long, thin snippets from both browns and build the heron's two "stick" legs.

6. Create reeds by cutting long (12″), thin snippets from each green fabric and place them throughout the water area.

7. Check to make sure all of the snippets are glue side down before fusing them permanently in place.

8. Add the borders, machine quilt, and bind.

You Will Need

Foundation Fabric
  White   36″ x 28″
Palette Fabrics
Panels:
  Light marbled pink (sky)
                                 36″ x 12″
  Light marbled gray
    (middle sky)   36″ x 12″
  Wine (mountains)   12″ x 6″
  Marbled blue (water)   36″ x 4″
  4 pinks   6″ x 6″ (each)
  Light grays   6″ x 6″ (each)
  2 light browns   4″ x 12″ (each)
  4 teal blues   12″ x 6″ (each)
  Gold   6″ x 6″
Steam-A-Seam2   7 yds.
Inner Border
Pink
                        Cut 2 strips: 2″ x 36″
                        Cut 2 strips: 2″ x 31″
Outer Border
  Dark teal
                        Cut 2 strips: 5″ x 39″
                        Cut 2 strips: 5″ x 40″
Backing Fabric   42″ x 50″
Binding Fabric   1/4 yd.
Cotton Batting   42″ x 50″

Wild Dolphins II*, 36″ x 44″, 1997, by Cindy Walter. Friends of mine who had an opportunity to swim with wild dolphins off the coast of Hawaii inspired this piece. The excitement they felt over their experience with these majestic creatures led me to create two Dolphin Snippet projects, both of which were featured in the original* Snippet Sensations. *I enjoyed making these projects because I used my favorite "stash" fabrics. Remember, this is your project; they do not have to be gray and the water does not have to be blue for your project to be successful. The silhouette patterns of each dolphin help with the construction and placement of each animal. Use them "as is" for a miniature project or enlarge them 200 percent for the full-size version.*

Project 23

Wild Dolphins II

1. Cut and iron the foundation fabric and pre-fuse the palette fabrics. In this project, the white foundation is completely covered with snippets. To create this project faster, and to use less fabric and web, you could alter these instructions and place the dolphins on a blue water-colored fabric as an exposed foundation.

2. Prepare the four dolphin silhouettes. Enlarge the patterns 200 percent if you want to create a project like this one, or, for a miniature project, use the patterns "as is" and reduce the supply list fabric amounts by one half. Collectively trace the dolphin shapes onto the paper side of a 12″ x 24″ piece of fusible web. *Do not overlap.* Pre-fuse the web to the piece of 12″ x 24″ white fabric. Cut out the white dolphin silhouettes and position them on the foundation fabric using the placement diagram provided (do not

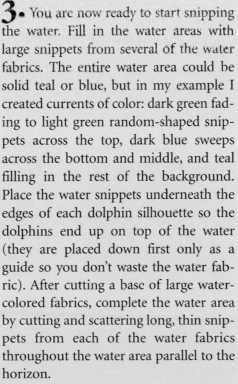

iron). The dolphins will not be filled in with snippets until later. Position them now as a placement guideline. The water snippets will go in the areas surrounding the silhouettes and will tuck under the dolphin bodies.

3. You are now ready to start snipping the water. Fill in the water areas with large snippets from several of the water fabrics. The entire water area could be solid teal or blue, but in my example I created currents of color: dark green fading to light green random-shaped snippets across the top, dark blue sweeps across the bottom and middle, and teal filling in the rest of the background. Place the water snippets underneath the edges of each dolphin silhouette so the dolphins end up on top of the water (they are placed down first only as a guide so you don't waste the water fabric). After cutting a base of large water-colored fabrics, complete the water area by cutting and scattering long, thin snippets from each of the water fabrics throughout the water area parallel to the horizon.

You Will Need

Foundation Fabric
  White   24″ x 32″
Dolphin silhouettes
  White   12″ x 42″
Palette Fabrics
Water:
  6 shades of teal, from light
    to dark   12″ x 12″ (each)
  4 shades of blue, from
    medium to dark
                    12″ x 12″ (each)
  3 shades of green, from light
    to dark   12″ x 12″ (each)
  2 shades of lavender
                    6″ x 6″ (each)
Dolphins:
  White (use leftover scraps from
    the silhouettes)
  Off-white   12″ x 6″
  Cream   6″ x 6″
  Tan   6″ x 6″
  Light brown   6″ x 6″
  Medium brown   6″ x 6″
  Dark brown   6″ x 6″
  Very dark brown/black   6″ x 6″
  Silver   6″ x 6″
  Light gray   6″ x 6″
  Medium blue-gray   6″ x 6″
  Dark blue-gray   6″ x 6
  Mauve   4″ x 6″
Steam-A-Seam2   8 yds.
Inner Border
  Tan print
            Cut 2 strips: 2″ x 32″
            Cut 2 strips: 2″ x 27″
Outer Border
  Blue-teal print
            Cut 2 strips: 5″ x 35″
            Cut 2 strips: 5″ x 36″
Backing Fabric   38″ x 46″
Binding Fabric   1/4 yd.
Cotton Batting   38″ x 46″

4. Check to make sure all of the water snippets and dolphin silhouette snippets are glue side down, and then fuse them to permanently set in place.

5. You are now ready to create the dolphins. Use my project as a guideline, keeping in mind that you can change the color scheme if desired. Start with the uppermost dolphin. Layer the top of its back and the top fin with dark blue and gray fabrics. Then, fill in the center portion with tans and the front top area with light blue-gray fabrics. Place beige and white snippets along the bottom of the dolphin. The inner fin is white on top, then beige, turning to tan on the bottom. The bottom fin is steel blue lined with thin brown snippets. Cut a long thin slit of very dark brown for the mouth and an oval for the eye.

6. Create the remaining dolphins in a similar manner (as described in Step 5), variegating color as desired.

7. Check to make sure all of the snippets are glue side down before fusing them permanently in place.

8. Add the borders, machine quilt, and bind.

Enlarge this pattern 200 percent for a full-size project, or, for a miniature project, use the patterns "as is."

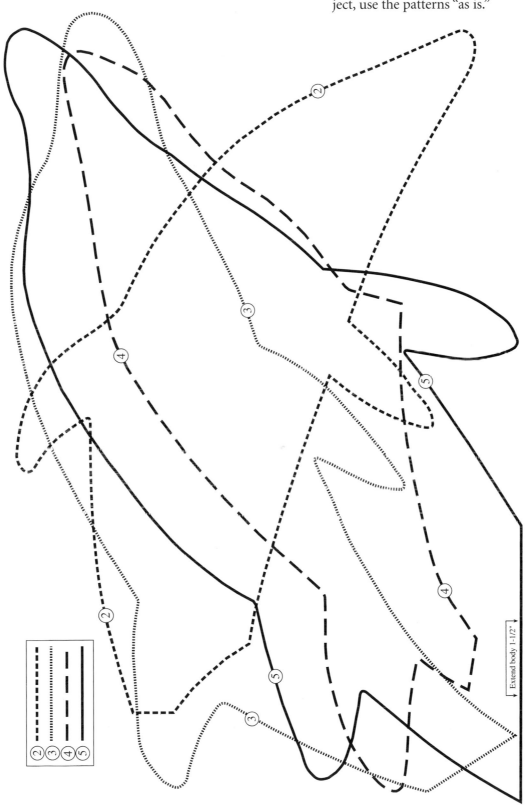

Extend body 1-1/2"

Suggested Reading

Becker, Joyce R. Nature's Press: *Inspiration and Techniques for Quilt Makers*. Quilt Digest Press. 1996.

Barber, Barbara. *Broderie Perse: The Elegant Quilt*. Paducah, KY: American Quilter's Society. 1997.

Drexler, Joyce. *Sulky Secrets to Successful Quilting*. Harbor Heights, FL: Sulky of America. 2000.

Hargrave, Harriet. *Heirloom Machine Quilting*. Lafayette, CA: C&T. 1995.

Lehman, Libby. *Threadplay*. Bothel, WA: That Patchwork Place. 1997.

Laporte, Gül. *Quilts from Europe: Projects and Inspiration*. Lafayette, CA: C&T. 2000.

Leone, Diana. *Crazy With Cotton*. Lafayette, CA: C&T. 1996.

Leone, Diana and Cindy Walter. *Attic Windows*, 2nd Ed. Iola, WI: Krause Publications. 2000.

Leone, Diana and Cindy Walter. *Fine Hand Quilting*, 2nd Ed. Iola, WI: Krause Publications. 2000.

Leone, Diana. *The New Sampler Quilt*. Lafayette, CA: C&T. 1996.

McClun, Diana and Laura Nownes. *Quilts!, Quilts!!, Quilts!!!* Lincolnwood, IL: Quilt Digest. 1997.

Noble, Maurine. *Decorative Threads*. Bothel, WA: That Patchwork Place. 1998.

Noble, Maurine. *Machine Quilting Made Easy*. Bothel, WA: That Patchwork Place. 1994.

QUILTER'S Newsletter Magazine. Leman Publications, Inc.

Walter, Cindy. *Snippet Sensations*. Iola, WI: Krause Publications. 1996.

Sources and Suppliers

For Seminars or lectures contact:

Cindy Walter
C/O Krause Publications
700 East State Street
Iola, WI 54990-0001
E-mail: snippetsensation@aol.com

Look for products from these companies wherever you buy quality sewing and quilting supplies.

Alaska Dyeworks
300 W. Swanson, #101
Wasilla, AK 99654
800-478-1755

Block Party Studios, Inc. (custom-made labels)
Jeanne Coverdale
922 L Ave.
Nevada, IA 50201
(515) 382-3150
E-mail: blockparty@nevia.net
www.blockpartystudios.com

Marilyn Doheny (lectures and teaching)
P.O. Box 1175
Edmonds, WA 98020
(425) 774-3761

Fabric to Dye For
2 River Rd.
Pawcatuck, CT 06379
888-322-1319
E-mail: todyefor@Riconnect.com
www.fabricstodyefor.com

Fiskars, Inc. (Softouch™ Multi-purpose scissors)
7811 West Stewart Ave.
Wausau, WI 54401

Mark Frey Photography (quilt and fiber art photography)
P.O. Box 1596
Yelm, WA 98597
(360) 894-3591
E-mail: markfrey@olywa.net

Husqvarna Viking Sewing Machines
31000 Viking Parkway
Weatlake, OH 44145-8012

Carol Ingram (textile art designer)
P.O. Box 483
Auburndale, FL 33823
E-mail: memawape@aol.com

Prym-Dritz Corp./Omnigrid
14 Westover Ave.
Slamford, CT 06902

Skydyes Fabric
P.O. Box 370116
West Hartford, CT 06137-00116
www.skydyes.com

Springs Industries/RHC
420 E. White St.
Rock Hill, SC 29730

Sulky of America
3113 Broadpoint Dr.
Harbor Heights, FL 33988

The Warm Company
(Steam-A-Seam2, Warm n' Natural batting)
954 E. Union St.
Seattle, WA 98122
206-320-9276

Timid Thimble (quilting gloves)
14298 E. Sprit Dr.
Westfield, IN 46076
www.timidthimble.com

Yellow Brick Road Patterns
Susan Smith
P.O. Box 72
Issaquah, WA 98027
(425) 391-4883
E-mail: villagequilter@sprintmail.com